BLACK LEADERSHIP:
BECOMING THE SUM

ElDon J. White

DEDICATION

To God

For saving my life, restoring my identity, shaping my purpose, guiding every step, and carrying me through seasons I was not strong enough to carry myself. Everything I have written, survived, learned, and become is evidence of Your grace, Your protection, and Your unwavering love. My entire journey is proof of Your faithfulness.

To my Agapi Mou, Dr. Laurine LeBlanc-White

You are my partner in purpose, my source of peace, and the strength that steadies me. Thank you for your prayers, your patience, your discernment, and the way you have always believed in my calling even when I struggled to see it clearly. You have sharpened my character and expanded my vision. Your love has shaped the man, the leader, and the father I have become. I love you endlessly.

To our children, Aamir, Elias, Matthew, Eden, Anya, ElDon II, Liya, and Luca

Each of you is a gift. Each of you carries destiny. Each of you reflects the goodness of God in a different way. You have taught me responsibility through your innocence, compassion through your need for guidance, humility through your questions, and purpose through your presence. I lead with intention because your eyes are watching. I grow with discipline because your futures depend on my example. I walk in purpose so you will know what it looks like to become everything God designed you to be. This book is part of my legacy, but you eight are my legacy. Everything I build is for you.

To my parents

Thank you for loving me through my best seasons and my hardest seasons. Your sacrifice and your support shaped a foundation I still stand on.

To my grandparents

Thank you for your sacrifices, legacy and love. I owe you the world.

To my aunts, uncles, cousins, siblings, and extended family

You are woven throughout my story. Thank you for your love, your influence, and the pieces of wisdom that helped form the man I became.

To my in-law family

Thank you for embracing me with acceptance, honor, and love.

To my friends, past leaders, and colleagues

Thank you for every lesson, every conversation, every challenge, and every moment that sharpened my growth. There is no version of me without the people who helped shape me.

THE SUM PREFACE

There comes a point in every leader's life when achievement is no longer enough to hide what's happening inside. You can lead people, serve teams, and accomplish things others admire, and still feel a gap inside your own identity. I lived in that gap for years. I carried pain I never named. I pushed through seasons I never healed. I built strength on top of survival and called it leadership because I didn't know anything else.

But leadership built on survival eventually collapses under its own weight.

The journey you're about to walk through isn't about strategies. It isn't about image. It isn't about leading people better so you can look more capable or confident. This journey is about identity. Not the identity the world gave you. Not the identity success demands. Not the identity struggle shaped.

It's the identity God always intended for you.

The **SUM - SEE+UNDERSTAND+MANIFEST** was born from the hardest seasons of my life. Seasons where I had to confront the truth that I couldn't outrun my past, outperform my wounds, or out-lead my broken identity. The SUM wasn't a theory. It was a lifeline. A path back to myself. A path back to clarity. A path back to purpose.

You're holding this book because something in you knows there is more. More truth. More alignment. More identity.

This book will not ask you to become someone new. It will ask you to become someone true.

The person God had in mind before the pain, before the mistakes, before the pressure, before the world tried to tell you who you were.

As you step into Part I, I want you to do something most leaders rarely do: slow down, breathe, and see yourself clearly. The version you protect. The version you keep quiet. The version that still matters.

Identity is the ground everything else grows from.
Let's begin there where every great leader is truly formed.

Before you move forward, take a moment. This is more than a book. It is an invitation to return to yourself with honesty, grace, and expectation.

HOW TO USE THIS BOOK

This book is not meant to be rushed or skimmed. It is designed to be experienced. Each chapter follows a rhythm that builds clarity, emotional truth, and leadership transformation.

Here's how to get the most from it:

1. Read one chapter at a time. Each chapter introduces a piece of your identity and leadership foundation. Give yourself space to absorb the message.

2. Use the SUM IT UP sections intentionally. These are transformation tools. SEE reveals the truth. UNDERSTAND reveals the meaning. MANIFEST reveals the action.

3. Journal your answers. Your breakthroughs will come from the questions, not the paragraphs.

4. Apply one insight each day. Leadership changes in small, consistent steps, not dramatic emotional moments.

5. Let the prayers settle you. They are grounding points. They align your identity with God's intention for you.

6. Do not rush the process.

This book is not a sprint. It is a return to yourself.

You will not be the same at the end.

THE SUM QUICK REFERENCE

SEE

What shaped me?

What patterns am I repeating?

What truth am I avoiding?

What strengths am I ignoring?

What identity have I accepted that is not mine?

UNDERSTAND

Why do I respond the way I do?

What beliefs drive my decisions?

What wounds have I normalized?

What strengths need development?

What is God revealing about who I am becoming?

MANIFEST

What do I need to embody now?

What actions align with my true identity?

What habits support the leader I am becoming?

What relationships and environments match my purpose?

What does alignment require from me today?

SUM in One Sentence:

Identity creates clarity. Clarity shapes decisions. Decisions manifest leadership.

"Great leaders are not defined by what they achieve, but by what they overcome."

CONTENTS

"Every wound has a lesson. Every lesson has a purpose. Every purpose has a leader."

PROLOGUE

"God Saved My Soul. Leadership Saved My Life."

I was seven years old the first time the world tried to break me. And at that age, you don't have the words for pain… you only have the feeling of it.

Heavy.

Confusing.

Suffocating.

Something inside me changed that day. Something was taken. And something else was born. From that moment at seven, there wasn't enough love in the world to make me feel protected again. So I did what many do:

I built walls.

Thick ones.

I harbored distrust. I nurtured anger.

I gave both of them a home inside me, because they felt safe.

By sixteen, those same emotions pushed me out of two different homes. I remember one night when the cold gripped me so violently that my body locked up. The wind cut through my clothes like it was trying to reach bone. I collapsed into a ditch just to get a moment of relief from the cold beating against my thin clothes and skin.

The ditch became my shield against the sharp needles.

My breath was the only warmth I could count on.

I felt low, but the ditch wasn't the bottom.

It was the beginning.

Because life wasn't done testing me.

Not even close.

Years later, I traded that cold ditch for the blistering heat of Afghanistan.

Where the air tasted like dust and metal.

Where every breath felt borrowed.

Where every step carried a question:

"Is this the one?"

I watched friends get blown apart by an enemy we couldn't see, and still we had to keep moving.

Step after step.

Heartbeat after heartbeat.

The dry earth crunching below my feet uncertain what the next step would bring.

Combat changes you.

It reveals you.

It strips away anything that isn't real.

It shows you who you are when everything around you is falling apart.

And somehow, through the trauma, the cold, the heat, the death, the silence... something in me refused to die. Instead, I learned to fight. I learned to keep getting up no matter what life or my choices brought to me. I was becoming a warrior. People see the leader I am today and think it came from discipline or training. Everything I have become as a leader is because I went back to SEE my pain.

To face it.

To heal it.

To grow from it.

To reclaim the parts of me that were buried under years of survival.

Leadership came from my willingness to confront my brokenness. To stop running from it. I am the leader I am because I refused to let the darkest moments of my past define the future God had for me. Because I learned that the only way to lead people is to first learn how to lead yourself out of the places that tried to destroy you.

Everything in this book was born from that journey.

And now, I'm handing it to you.

You have the ability to break through.

To rise.

Every leader must learn to SEE.

See your story.

See your truth.

See the moments that shaped you.

See the pieces that tried to break you.

See the strength you refused to let go.

Only then can you Understand.

Only then can you Manifest.

Only then can you become the Sum.

To become the sum of every battle you refused to lose. I am proof of that. Let my story become your roadmap to an undeniable future. Let this be the moment you stop running from who you were and step into who you were always meant to be.

Greatness isn't found.

Greatness is forged.

And this, right here, right now is where your becoming begins.

"Before you lead the world, you must confront the world within."

INTRODUCTION

THE SUM OF WHO YOU BECAME

There are moments in life when you realize the version of yourself that the world sees is not the same one you live with. You can be admired, accomplished, disciplined, or even feared, and still feel a fracture inside that no one else recognizes. Leadership books rarely start in that place. They begin with strategies and principles, as if leadership begins polished.

But real leadership does not begin polished.

It begins in the shadows of the parts of your story that you have avoided.

The parts that shaped you long before anyone knew your name.

For years, I lived as two versions of myself. The one people saw, and the one I kept hidden. Outwardly, I was capable, focused, and driven. Inside, I was tired, conflicted, and quietly unraveling. I learned how to perform strength well enough that no one questioned whether I was struggling. I learned how to push hard enough that no one noticed where I was hurting. And I learned how to achieve enough that no one suspected the weight I carried when the uniform came off.

That duality is far more common than most people will ever admit, and it creates a widening gap inside a leader.

We live in a world that praises resilience but rarely acknowledges what it costs. We celebrate perseverance without examining the wounds underneath. We applaud strength but remain silent about the breaking it required. And because of that silence, many people mistake survival for leadership. They confuse endurance with purpose. They confuse numbness with discipline.

I wrote this book because I reached a point where survival was no longer enough. I had succeeded in ways I once dreamed about. I had earned titles, completed missions, and stepped into roles that demanded precision and grit. Yet even as I excelled outwardly, my inner world grew darker and quieter. I felt disconnected from myself, a stranger wearing my own life.

At some point, you stop asking whether you can keep going.

You start asking why you are going at all.

That question changed everything.

The journey to answer it became the foundation of this book. Leadership, for me, was not born from triumph. It was born from truth. Not from titles. From honesty. Not from strength alone. From healing. Healing began when I was finally willing to see my story clearly and stop pretending I was unaffected by it. I didn't know it then, but I was stepping into the first pillar of what I now call the SUM Model: See.

And to understand where that journey began, you have to go back further than the uniform, or the missions, or the moments people think define leadership. You have to go back to a sixteen-year-old boy standing at a Greyhound station with a one-way ticket to Ypsilanti, Michigan.

My friends thought I was leaving to chase sports. They believed I was hungry for opportunity. The truth was far less heroic. I was broken. I carried a face that looked emotionless on the outside but was flooded with confusion on the inside. I was angry in ways I couldn't explain, because anger was the only emotion I knew how to access. What I didn't realize then was that the anger was not anger at all. It was hurt. Hurt that I didn't know how to name. Hurt that started the day I was molested at seven years old by people trusted to protect me. Hurt from the confusion of loving parents while navigating the absence of a biological father who didn't know how to love me back. Hurt layered on top of a birth that began with a fight. My mother battling cancer while carrying me, my body entering the world blue, breathless, and wrapped in the cord that gave me life and also nearly took my life.

The battles began early. And they kept coming.

Ypsilanti was supposed to be a fresh start, but it became a harsher classroom than I could have imagined. I slept on a couch and lived out of a suitcase. I washed the same few clothes repeatedly because the family dog used them as a daily bathroom spot. I walked home from practices in weather that felt cruel. And on the day my pain finally erupted into anger, I was put out into the cold.

That night, I wandered the streets with nowhere to go. I knocked on doors of friends who would not let me in. I curled up in a ditch to shield myself from the wind. Another night, a neighbor let me sleep in a den crowded with dogs, and I woke up covered in flea bites.

I was hungry.

I was cold.

I was exhausted.

I was confused.

I was hurt.

And I did not know how to process any of it.

But something happened to me in those moments... something that would shape the rest of my life. After spending so much time low, so much time angry, so much time feeling invisible, something inside me began to shift. My anger softened into awareness. My bitterness broke open into reflection. My survival instincts cracked enough for empathy to emerge.

I realized the world did not owe me healing.

I had to participate as if I owed myself.

I needed to become the person I wished had shown up for me.

I needed to stop giving my pain permission to lead me.

I needed to stop excusing behavior and start examining it.

I needed strength, yes, but I also needed forgiveness, courage, humility, and God.

In that transformation, I found the first truth of leadership:

Before you can lead anyone else, you must learn to lead yourself.

And leading yourself starts with confronting the parts of you that you have allowed to remain unled. The unspoken wounds, the hidden insecurities, the stories you keep buried because naming them feels like weakness. Leadership does not start with ambition. It starts with honesty. It starts with seeing your story as it really is. This is the beginning of SUM The moment when See becomes the doorway to everything else.

Many people never reach their potential not because they lack talent, but because their foundation was never strengthened. They try to climb while their inner world collapses. They try to influence others while avoiding the truth of who they are becoming. And eventually, the gap between their public image and private identity becomes too wide to sustain.

That gap nearly cost me everything.

Not because I was incapable, but because I was incomplete.

When I say leadership saved my life, I do not mean the kind found in manuals. I mean the kind that forces you to rebuild your relationship with your own soul. The kind that makes you confront the silence you've avoided. The kind that teaches you that strength is not the absence of pain but the transformation of it.

And this is where the idea of Black Leadership and Becoming the Sum enters the heart of this book.

Black, in its truest form, is not an absence. It is an absorption. Black gathers every wavelength of light into itself. It holds complexity. It holds depth. It holds history and presence. Black does not reflect. It collects. It carries. Leadership, at its highest level, works the same way.

You are not shaped by one story.

You are shaped by the sum of them.

Your failures and your victories.

Your fractures and your resilience.

Your trauma and your transformation.

Your identity, your faith, your perspective, your grit, your gifts.

Leadership is the absorption of all your moments into wisdom.

And this is the bridge into the SUM Model.

The journey that took me years to understand now comes down to three movements:

SEE. UNDERSTAND. MANIFEST.

You Must See.

See your truth with honesty.

See your truth without running

See the patterns and wounds you have carried.

See the strength you forgot was yours.

You Must Understand.

Understand what shapes you.

Understand where healing is needed.

Understand the identity beneath your survival.

Understand the purpose behind your pain.

You Must Manifest.

Manifest a new identity.

Manifest disciplined leadership.

Manifest purpose through action.

Manifest the life God has been calling you toward.

This is the leadership that embraces depth instead of perfection. Identity instead of performance. Truth instead of image. Leadership that understands you cannot rise fully until you stop hiding the parts of you that feel least worthy of the climb.

You are not reading a story of perfection.

You are entering a journey of transformation.

And transformation begins when you decide that you will no longer settle for the version of yourself built for survival.

You are stepping into the version that leadership requires. The version that absorbs every part of your story and transforms it into strength.

This is where your becoming begins.

Turn the page.

THE SUM MODEL: The Framework of Black Leadership

SEE + UNDERSTAND + MANIFEST

1. SEE
See your story clearly.
See the truth beyond the pain.
See your gifts, your patterns, your identity.
See the good, the hard, the hidden.
This is where leadership starts: not with action, but with awareness.

2. UNDERSTAND
Understand the meaning behind every moment.
Understand your identity, your healing, your emotional rhythm.
Understand the purpose behind your pressure, the weight behind your wisdom.
Before you lead anyone else, understand the landscape within yourself.

3. MANIFEST
Manifest your leadership outwardly.
Manifest purpose through presence, influence, clarity, and discipline.
Manifest legacy through people, through culture, through calling.
Leadership is not the performance of strength, it is the manifestation of identity.

This is Black Leadership.

This is Becoming the Sum.
This is the SUM Model.

SEE+UNDERSTAND+MANIFEST

ElDon J. White

PART I

THE FOUNDATION OF BECOMING THE SUM

"Pressure is the classroom. Experience is the teacher. Becoming is the assignment."

CHAPTER 1

THE FORGE OF EXPERIENCE

You do not become a leader the day someone hands you a title. You do not become a leader the day you receive a promotion, a rank, or a new set of responsibilities. Leadership begins long before any of that. It begins in the moments you would rather forget, in the places where pain shapes you faster than progress, and in the seasons where life demands something from you that you are not yet convinced you possess.

For most of my life, I did not understand this. I thought leadership was about strength that people could see from a distance. I thought it was about composure that never cracked, confidence that never wavered, and decisiveness that never hesitated. I thought leadership was something you learned to display, not something you learned to confront within yourself. I thought leadership was earned through achievement, not survival.

Then life, in its unrelenting way, taught me the truth.

Leadership revealed itself to me on a night when I was sitting alone on the edge of my bunk, deployed overseas, holding a nine millimeter Beretta in my hand. The room was dark. The air felt thick and unmoving, as if the entire world had frozen around me. My uniform clung to my skin with the weight of exhaustion that had nothing to do with the mission. My thoughts had become heavier than my body. And for the first time in my life, it felt as if my mind no longer belonged to me.

I remember the coldness of the steel in my hand. It shocked me at first, like a truth I had been avoiding. I remember how the bullet felt in my right hand. I remember thinking that the world might be better without me in it. I remember wondering when exactly I had begun to disappear from myself, when the version of me I once recognized had slipped into silence. There was no noise outside. No chaos. No combat. Just the sound of my own breathing and a heart that felt like it had stopped believing in me.

No one came knocking.

No one came looking.

No one came to save me from myself.

Pain becomes dangerous when it grows quiet. Loud pain forces you to fight. Quiet pain convinces you that you are already defeated. Quiet pain whispers that there is no point. That night, the silence inside me felt final.

I raised the empty weapon to my head. My hand trembled from the confusion of not understanding myself anymore. I had survived explosions. I had survived long missions, long nights, combat stress, and emotional turmoil. But I had not survived my own mind. And I did not know how.

Before I finished squeezing the trigger, something rose inside me. It was not strength. It was not clarity. It was a sudden fear of the truth. I realized I did not want to die. I wanted the pain to stop. I wanted the numbness to break. I wanted to feel something again, something real, something hopeful. But in that moment, all I could feel was the cold steel and the weight of surrender.

The click echoed through the room like a command. It was louder than any explosion I had survived. Louder than any briefing I had attended. Louder than any fear I had tried to bury. That sound did not free me. It confronted me. It forced a truth I had spent years avoiding.

No one was coming to rescue me.

If I wanted to live, I had to lead myself out of the darkness I had become comfortable in.

Self leadership does not begin with motivation. It does not begin with confidence. It begins with honesty. It begins with the willingness to look at your own pain, acknowledge it without shielding yourself, and decide that you are worth the work required to rise again. I had never been taught that. I had only been taught how to survive externally. I had never been taught how to survive internally.

That night did not turn me into a leader. It exposed the part of me that had never been led. It showed me that the greatest battlefield I would ever face was the one no one else could see.

I spent years leading teams in high risk environments. I had given direction. I had made decisions. I had executed missions that required precision and clarity. Yet in my quietest moment, the one person I had never learned to lead was myself. That realization broke me in ways no deployment ever could. It forced me to confront the version of myself I had avoided. It forced me to accept that leadership begins with the person you see in the mirror before it ever reaches anyone else.

Healing became my first act of leadership.

Honesty became my first challenge.

Vulnerability became my first weapon.

Growth became my first assignment.

Transformation did not happen quickly. It did not happen cleanly. It did not come with a single prayer, a single conversation, or a single moment of clarity. It came through small decisions. It came through admitting things I did not want to say aloud. It came through learning to ask for help. It came through conversations that hurt but healed. It came through learning to forgive myself for things I never should have been holding against myself.

Somewhere in the process, I realized that every leader people admire has walked through something that nearly broke them. Some survived families that abandoned them. Some survived the weight of responsibility they were not prepared for. Some survived their own doubt, their own failure, their own silence. Some, like me, survived their own minds.

Leadership begins in the fire.

Transformation begins in the breaking.

Purpose begins in the moment you decide you are worth rebuilding.

The world sees the medals, the titles, the promotions. It rarely sees the nights you begged God for one more reason to stay. Yet those nights are often where leadership is truly born.

When I say that God saved my soul but leadership saved my life, it is because leadership forced me to confront what I had avoided. Leadership demanded accountability. It demanded responsibility. It demanded emotional courage. It demanded a willingness to walk toward the parts of myself I did not understand. It demanded that I become the person others needed me to be, but also the person I needed to become for myself.

Leadership did not begin the moment others followed me.

Leadership began the moment I decided to stop abandoning myself.

And I didn't decide that until after a long 15 month deployment. Coming home after a long deployment felt like stepping into a world I no longer recognized. The colors looked too bright, as if someone had adjusted the contrast on reality. The sounds felt louder, sharper, and intrusive. Even the air felt foreign. I had turned twenty one in Iraq, surrounded by violence, indirect fire, long nights, missions that blurred together, and a sense of purpose that existed only because survival depended on it. There is a unique kind of clarity that comes from living in an environment where every moment matters. Returning to a place where the world moved without me felt disorienting.

When the buses pulled up to the parade field, the atmosphere exploded with celebration. Families rushed forward with tears and laughter. Children ran into waiting arms. Flags waved. The band played. Signs with names and welcome home messages bounced above the crowd. It was a reunion filled with emotion, but it was a reunion I did not know how to participate in. I watched Soldiers fall into the arms of the people who belonged to them. I watched relief wash over the faces of parents and spouses. And I stood in formation feeling like a visitor in my own life.

Halfway through the deployment I had received a Dear John letter. I told myself it did not matter. I told myself I had expected it. I told myself I did not need anyone. But standing there surrounded by reunions I was not part of, the truth hit harder than any blast I had felt overseas. I felt abandoned. I felt forgotten. I felt like I had returned to a world that had no place ready for me.

Because I was still married, and had not yet had the opportunity to file the divorce, I was not allowed back in the barracks. Regulations did not consider emotional reality. They only recognized paperwork. At the duplex I had rented before deploying, an eviction notice was taped to the door. My belongings were gone. The lock had been changed. At least I had the courtesy of knowing this before I left that parade field. I stood there in uniform with a duffel bag at my feet, staring at a piece of paper that confirmed what I had already felt.

I was home, but I had nowhere to go.

People talk about the loneliness of deployment, but they rarely talk about the loneliness of returning. They do not talk about the feeling of walking from combat into a place where everyone expects you to be fine. They do not talk about the emptiness that follows you when the adrenaline disappears. They do not talk about the silence that comes after months of constant noise.

As I stood there, a friend approached me. He was not overly emotional. He did not try to hug me or give some inspirational speech. He simply walked over, looked me in the eyes, and asked, "You good?"

I nodded even though everything inside me said no.

He asked if I had somewhere to go. I told him I did not. He did not ask another question. He did not pressure me. He did not make me explain. He reached into his pocket, pulled out a set of keys, and said, "I have a unit open in one of my fourplexes. Use it until you get back on your feet."

No conditions.

No expectations.

No judgment.

It was quiet leadership. The kind that comes from someone who understands that words are not always the answer. Sometimes presence is enough.

That one act did not erase my pain, but it reminded me of something I had started to forget. I was not disposable. My life still had weight. My story still had value. And even when I felt unseen, God could still send people who saw what I could not see in myself.

I moved into that small apartment that night. It was empty except for the basics. A mattress. A chair. A table. But it felt like a lifeline. It gave me a place to breathe again. At night, I would sit in the chair by the window and stare at the parking lot lights. I felt suspended between two lives. I had survived fifteen months in Iraq, but I had not returned whole.

There were moments when I would sit on the floor with my back against the wall, feeling the weight of everything I had experienced pressing against me. I questioned who I was supposed to be now. I questioned whether I still had purpose. I questioned whether the world had moved on without me. I questioned whether coming home was supposed to feel this confusing.

But in that confusion, something became clear.

I could not stay who I was.

I did not know what the next version of me should look like, but I knew the current version could not carry me forward. I needed direction. I needed challenge.

I needed something that forced me to evolve.

That apartment became the place where I started to rebuild myself. Not quickly, not neatly, but honestly. It was the first place I realized that transformation begins long before the world notices. It begins in the silence when you decide you cannot remain the same.

The nights were long, but the clarity they brought was real. I needed something bigger than routine. I needed a mission that demanded more from me. Not so I could prove anything to anyone else, but so I could remember who I was capable of becoming.

That desire led me down a path that would reshape my identity in ways I did not expect. It would push me beyond my limits, correct my view of myself, and forge the leader I would one day become.

It started with a simple thought:

"I cannot stay here. I have to become something more."

And that thought became the doorway to a journey I was not prepared for, but desperately needed.

The problem with returning from war is that your body arrives long before your mind does. You try to blend in. You try to move through rooms and conversations like you used to. You try to respond to questions the way people expect you to. But normal life feels like a jacket that no longer fits. You tug at the sleeves, you shift your shoulders, but you cannot settle into it.

During that deployment, indirect fire became part of the rhythm of our days. Mortars fell without warning. Rockets whistled in the distance. Dust clouds rose from impacts that shook the ground and rattled the walls. Even when the blasts were far away, the vibration traveled through the earth and into your bones. You learned to read the silence between explosions as carefully as the noise itself.

My job mattered, but it kept me inside more often than not. I produced intelligence. I created products that shaped missions. I contributed in ways that were essential but indirect. And there were nights when teams went out without me. Nights with updates about firefights, casualties, or success. Nights when I sat behind a computer while others ran toward danger.

A friend of mine was killed on that deployment. The news hit like a punch that knocked the wind out of me. It wasn't logical, but logic rarely survives grief. I kept replaying everything I could have done differently. I convinced myself that I had not earned the same right to be broken because I had lived while others had not. That guilt sat inside me like a stone. It did not speak loudly, but it was heavy enough that my steps changed.

I returned home with a silent conviction. I could not remain who I had been. I needed something more demanding. Something that would take every part of me and reshape it. Something that would force me to grow or expose the places where I still needed to heal.

The path I chose was not glamorous. It was not strategic. It was not even well planned. It was driven by something deeper. I wanted to become someone who would never again feel detached from the mission. I wanted to shoulder the weight alongside the men who had inspired me. I wanted to step into arenas that scared me. I wanted to feel alive again.

That is how the 75th Ranger Regiment became the next step.

I was not chasing prestige. I was not thinking about being the first geospatial engineer in Regiment history. At that time, the historical significance meant nothing to me. I wasn't even aware it existed. I was chasing purpose. I was looking for something that could either break me or rebuild me. And I was ready for either outcome.

On paper, it looked like a career move. In reality, it was a soul decision. I was volunteering for a forge that would test every story I believed about myself.

Selection demanded everything. Every step. Every breath. Every doubt. The cold mornings started before sunrise, the kind of cold that bites into your skin and makes it feel like your muscles are shrinking. The rucks dragged on until time lost meaning. The straps cut into your shoulders. Your feet swelled. Blisters formed under your toenails. The weight shifted unpredictably, and you learned quickly that your mind quit before your body did.

The land navigation phases took you into terrain that tested not just your skills, but your patience with yourself. You were tired. You were hungry. You were dragging your gear through mud, brush, and steep climbs. And as the hours dragged on, your thoughts became your only companion. Some men argued with themselves. Some cursed the ground they walked on. Some quieted down because they knew that the longer they listened to their mind, the more dangerous it became.

Every man hit a moment where quitting felt easier than finding the next checkpoint. And every man had to face the fact that no one was coming to carry them through it. You either found the next point or the process ended for you.

In less than two weeks into selection, over 100 men from our class of 207 quit.. What kept me moving was the simple truth that going back to the version of myself I had been was no longer an option. I could not return to a life where I felt stuck inside my own skin. I could not return to the emotional numbness that had nearly taken my life. I needed this. I needed a reason to believe I could still become someone worth following.

Every step in that process chipped away at the parts of me I no longer needed. Every long night stripped another layer of fear. Every day of training revealed another layer of resilience I did not know I had. And the quiet moments between the exhaustion and the doubt became the places where I began to understand something important. Growth is not loud. It does not announce itself. It does not feel inspirational when you are inside it. It feels like work, pain, and uncertainty.

But looking back, that phase of my life became one of the purest forms of growth I have ever experienced. It forced me to confront who I had been, who I was becoming, and who I refused to remain.

When I finally earned my place in Regiment, there was no celebration. No one shook my hand and said I had made history. No banners. No recognition. I did not feel like I had arrived. I felt like I had begun. What mattered most to me in that moment was not the achievement but the transformation.

I had chosen the harder path not to escape myself, but to become someone new.

The first time I wore that scroll and tan beret felt like a quiet acknowledgment of a promise I had made in the darkness of that deployment. A promise to become a man who could lead himself before he tried to lead anyone else.

Ranger Regiment did not heal me. It forged me. It showed me discipline not as punishment, but as freedom. It taught me precision not as pressure, but as respect. It taught me brotherhood not as sentiment, but as sacrifice. And it taught me that leadership is not something you demonstrate when others are watching. It is something you live when no one is around to applaud you.

Regiment did not give me a title. It gave me identity. It gave me resilience. It gave me a sense of direction that had been missing. It gave me the space to become someone stronger, more grounded, and more aware of the responsibility that comes with influence.

The greatest lesson the Regiment taught me was this. Leadership is not built in the moment you are needed. It is built in the moments when you choose to prepare yourself to be needed.

Ranger Regiment reshaped the way I understood myself. The standard was not something you reached once and then held onto. The standard was something you lived. Every day. Every moment. You learned quickly that discipline was not punishment. It was a structure that protected excellence. It was the framework that allowed potential to become performance. It was the foundation of a culture where everyone understood that their actions affected the man to their left and their right.

In Regiment, you could not hide behind potential. You either lived the standard or you did not. There was no pretending to be prepared. The environment revealed whether you had done the work. It showed the truth of who you were when the pressure mounted, when fatigue blurred your vision, and when doubt tried to take hold. The truth was never loud. It was shown in the small decisions. The way you maintained your gear. The way you spoke. The way you carried yourself. The way you responded when things went wrong. Every detail mattered because every detail affected the mission.

It was the first time in my life where I felt all the different parts of me being shaped at once. My character was sharpened. My discipline was deepened. My resilience was solidified. And my purpose grew clearer through every repetition, every challenge, and every quiet moment where I had to choose whether I would rise or remain the same.

There were nights when we prepared for mission after mission, and the exhaustion hung on us like additional weight. Men who had lost sleep, lost time, and lost pieces of themselves still showed up because the brotherhood demanded it. I saw men push past pain that would have stopped others. I saw leadership demonstrated without words. I saw courage in the smallest actions, not just the biggest ones.

And in those moments, I began to understand something about leadership that I had not realized before. Leadership is not about being at the front. Leadership is about being willing to carry what others cannot. It is about stepping into responsibility that others might fear. It is about showing up when you feel empty and giving what you have because someone else depends on you.

Leadership is not the ability to move people. It is the ability to move yourself first.

Regiment taught me that leadership is built privately and revealed publicly. It is shaped in decisions no one applauds. It is strengthened in moments no one sees. It is proven in choices that do come with recognition. You do not rise to the level of the situation. You rise to the level of your preparation. And that preparation happens long before the world ever watches.

Over time, something else shifted in me. My view of myself changed. My understanding of responsibility changed. The way I carried my pain changed. I stopped seeing my past as a weight and began seeing it as material. I stopped viewing my experiences as barriers and began viewing them as the foundation of my character. The pieces of my life that had once felt like fractures became the places where strength was formed.

The breaking had not been a sign of weakness. It had been the beginning of transformation.

By the time I reached the midpoint of my career, I began to realize that everything I had survived had become the very things that prepared me for leadership. The dark moments, the confusing transitions, the loneliness, the guilt, the fear, the moments where hope felt like a distant concept, all became part of the man I was becoming. And through each stage of becoming, leadership began to take on a different meaning.

Leadership was not authority. It was responsibility.

Leadership was not perfection. It was honesty.

Leadership was not confidence. It was growth.

Leadership was not influence. It was integrity.

Leadership was not being followed. It was being consistent.

Leadership was not about the moment. It was about the work long before the moment.

The forge of experience had shaped me in ways I had not understood at the time. It took the night with the Beretta. It took the empty apartment. It took the guilt from Iraq. It took the grief of losing brothers. It took the cold nights of selection. It took the discipline of the Regiment. It took the internal battles no one knew about. It took each of those moments and used them to craft someone capable of carrying weight I once thought would crush me.

And something else happened during this time. I began to notice the patterns in people. I began to understand the emotional pulse of the teams I led. I began to recognize fear before it became failure. I began to see when someone needed a push versus when they needed patience. I began to hear the unspoken things that people tried to hide. I began to understand that leadership is not simply about directing actions. It is about understanding people.

You cannot lead people if you cannot feel them. You cannot feel people if you cannot first feel yourself. And you cannot feel yourself if you are not willing to confront the truth of who you are beneath the exterior.

The journey did not end in Regiment. It only began there. It set the foundation for a career that would require every lesson I had learned, every scar I carried, every moment of doubt I survived, and every moment of courage I had chosen even when I felt empty. Leadership became the lens through which I saw everything. It became the measure of every decision. It became the reason I pushed forward, even in seasons where I felt the weight of responsibility press against me with new intensity.

Years later, I realized the truth that had been forming all along. The uniform was never the source of my identity. The rank was never the source of my authority. The missions were never the source of my purpose. The experiences were shaping me, but they were not defining me. What defined me was the decision I made years before. The decision to live. The decision to lead myself. The decision to rise.

Leadership saved my life because leadership forced me into becoming the person I had always needed to be. It demanded healing. It demanded growth. It demanded transformation. It demanded courage long before courage felt natural.

If there is one thing I hope readers understand at the beginning of this book, it is this. Your journey will not make sense while you are still walking through it. But the moments that feel like breaking are often the moments that prepare you for black leadership and becoming the sum. Leadership does not begin with influence. It begins with survival. It begins with truth. It begins with the willingness to rise when everything inside you tells you to remain on the ground.

The forge of experience shaped me into someone who could lead.

Your forge may not look like mine. It may be a broken home, a failing marriage, a silent battle with anxiety, the weight of being the one everyone depends on, or a dream that keeps getting delayed. Whatever it is, do not dismiss it. The forge you are standing in right now is the very place where the leader inside you is being formed.

Chapter 1 SUM IT UP

THE SUM FRAMEWORK: SEE + UNDERSTAND + MANIFEST

Your story has weight. When you face it with honesty, it becomes strength.

SEE: the moments that tried to break you.

UNDERSTAND: how those moments shaped your identity and discipline.

MANIFEST: strength by owning your story with confidence.

BECOMING THE SUM:

1. What part of your story needs your honest attention?

2. How has this shaped your leadership?

3. What choice today reflects the strength you gained?

THE SUM CHALLENGE:

Write one truth about your past that you are ready to accept.

PRAYER FOR THE JOURNEY:

God, help me see my story with clarity and honor the strength You built in me. Amen.

"Identity rest in the journey of discovery and reclaiming."

CHAPTER 2

THE WEIGHT YOU CARRY

Every person carries a weight long before they know how to name it. Some of it comes from experiences that happened too early. Some comes from expectations quietly placed on your shoulders. Some comes from silence that stretched too long. And some comes from emotions you never learned to express. Whatever the source, the weight settles into your identity. It becomes a language you learn to speak without realizing it. It shapes your posture, your reactions, and the way you navigate the world.

Most people assume this weight is simply part of life. They grow accustomed to the tension in their chest or the uneasiness that rises in moments that should feel peaceful. They treat the heaviness like normalcy, believing it is what adulthood requires.

They interpret their drive as ambition, unaware that much of it began as a response to hurt rather than a desire to grow.

Leadership often begins this way.

Not with vision, but with burden.

Not with clarity, but with confusion.

Not with purpose, but with pressure.

Before you can become the leader you are meant to be, you must understand the weight you carry. Because if you never identify it, you will place it in every environment you enter. You will carry it into relationships, opportunities, responsibilities, and eventually into the people you lead.

UNEXAMINED IDENTITY

One of the first weights I carried came from the complexity of identity. Growing up with a biological father who remained distant creates a set of questions no child is prepared to answer. You do not understand adult relationships at that age. You only understand presence and absence. And when absence is your reality, it often transforms into a quiet belief that something must be wrong with you.

Even though I was deeply loved by my mother and father, that early gap left an imprint. You can be surrounded by love and still feel shaped by the one place it did not reach. Love can be consistent, yet questions can still linger beneath the surface. Contradicting realities create internal conflict. And when you are young, you try to reconcile the contradictions by building explanations that feel like truth, even when they are not.

Identity becomes something you construct from pieces rather than something you grow into naturally. And the weight of that construction follows you until you decide to examine it.

This is the first step of the SUM Model. Before you can Understand or Manifest anything, you must See what shaped you.

THE HABIT OF SILENCE

Another weight that shaped me was silence. Silence is a powerful teacher, but not always a healthy one. It trains you to keep emotions inside and pretend everything is fine. It teaches you to cope instead of connect. It conditions you to solve your own problems because involving others feels inconvenient or unsafe. It convinces you that vulnerability is a liability rather than a pathway to connection.

Over time, silence becomes second nature. You stop expecting to be understood and start believing that carrying more than your share is simply who you are. People praise your maturity without recognizing it was born from necessity, not choice. They admire your calm without seeing the storms you manage internally.

This pattern does not break easily. It follows you into adulthood and eventually into leadership. You become dependable to others and invisible to yourself.

THE MISINTERPRETATION OF HURT

Growing up, I misinterpreted hurt as anger. Anger was louder and easier to express. Hurt was confusing and harder to articulate. Anger felt powerful, even when it was misplaced. Hurt made me feel exposed. And without realizing it, I let anger protect the parts of me that were not yet healed.

What I did not understand was that hurt, when suppressed, does not disappear. It reappears in reactions you cannot explain. It shows up in moments of overreaction or emotional withdrawal. It interrupts relationships and undermines confidence. The struggles you endure early in life often become the weight you carry into your future unless you learn how to process them.

Leaders who carry unprocessed hurt often react rather than respond. They become overly disciplined or overly detached. They avoid conflict or invite it without realizing why. These patterns are not signs of weakness. They are signs of unexamined pain.

THE QUIET MOMENT THAT REVEALS EVERYTHING

Transformation rarely begins in dramatic moments. It usually begins in the quiet ones. I remember one of those moments clearly, long before adulthood or the military. I was walking home in the cold during my time in Ypsilanti, hands deep in my pockets, breath rising in small clouds. The environment was harsh, and so was my internal world. For most of my life, anger had been my companion. But that night, something shifted. My anger did not rise to the surface. Something softer did.

For the first time, I understood that I was not angry at the world. I was hurting inside it. I was not weak. I was exhausted. I was not lost. I was grieving parts of myself I never had the space to acknowledge.

Awareness does not fix pain instantly, but it changes your direction.

It creates the first crack in the armor you built to survive.

This was the moment I began to See myself honestly. The S in SUM is not about insight. It is about courage.

THE SHIFT TOWARD HONESTY

When you realize the weight you carry, you begin to see how it shapes your decisions. You recognize patterns you never questioned before. You pay attention to the moments that trigger reactions you do not understand. You become more aware of the beliefs you formed in childhood that still influence your adulthood.

This awareness is the beginning of transformation.

You learn that growth requires truth.

You learn that healing requires courage.

You learn that leadership requires vulnerability.

The weight you carry becomes less intimidating once you decide to confront it. Not because it disappears, but because you finally stop fighting it alone.

Seeing creates Understanding. Understanding creates choice. Choice creates transformation.

BECOMING THE STRONG ONE TOO SOON

Many people become the strong one in their family or environment long before they understand what strength truly is. I became that person early at 18. I was the one who held things together, the one people relied on, the one who tried to control his inner world to keep the outer world steady. But strength that is shaped too early becomes rigidity. You forget how to ask for help. You forget how to rest. You forget that strength without support becomes strain.

Being the strong one is not inherently harmful. It becomes harmful when strength is used to hide rather than to grow. And that is the point many leaders reach before they realize something must change.

THE WEIGHT YOU CARRY INTO LEADERSHIP

By the time people step into leadership, they are often operating from patterns formed long before they understood themselves. These patterns influence whether they listen or react, whether they trust or withdraw, whether they lead with empathy or with defensiveness.

Unexamined weight often shows up as:

• reluctance to delegate

• overworking to avoid stillness

• misinterpreting feedback as rejection

- emotional withdrawal under pressure
- performance being tied to identity
- difficulty creating boundaries
- fear of vulnerability
- chasing validation through achievement

These patterns do not come from lack of skill. They come from lack of understanding. They come from trying to lead with parts of yourself that were built for survival rather than growth.

THE TRANSFORMATION OF WEIGHT INTO WISDOM

When you finally confront the truth of what you carry, something shifts. The weight does not vanish. Instead, it becomes a lens through which you understand yourself with greater clarity. You learn what shaped you. You learn why you react the way you do. You learn what needs to be healed rather than hidden. And that understanding becomes the birthplace of empathy.

Empathy is not a soft trait. It is a precise one. It gives you the ability to interpret people, not just manage them. It gives you patience where judgment once lived. It gives you compassion where frustration used to dominate. It gives you perspective that can only come from honest self-reflection.

Wisdom is weight that has been processed.

Strength is weight that has been transformed.

Leadership is weight that has been repurposed.

THE POWER OF THE SUM

Your story is not defined by one experience. It is defined by the sum of them. Leadership is not shaped by a single victory or a single hardship. It is shaped by every lesson, every scar, every moment of growth, and every moment of becoming.

Black Leadership, as presented in this book, is rooted in the idea that leadership is the absorption of all your experiences. Just as the color black holds every wavelength of light, a leader holds every lesson from their past, shaping wisdom that others can benefit from.

This is the SUM in motion.

See what shaped you.

Understand why it matters.

Manifest who you are becoming.

The weight you carry does not diminish your potential. If understood, it becomes the foundation of your purpose. It becomes the reason you can understand people deeply, lead people responsibly, and rise beyond the limitations of your past.

This chapter is your invitation to examine the weight you carry without judgment. To see it not as evidence of weakness, but as the beginning of strength. To recognize that becoming a leader does not require an unblemished story. It requires an honest one.

Your story is not finished.

The weight is not the end.

It is the beginning of becoming.

Chapter 2 SUM IT UP

THE SUM FRAMEWORK: SEE + UNDERSTAND + MANIFEST

Every weight you carried taught you something. Honor the lesson.

SEE: the responsibilities that shaped you.

UNDERSTAND: how they influenced your thinking and leadership.

MANIFEST: release by no longer carrying what was never yours.

BECOMING THE SUM:

1. What weight have you carried too long?

2. How has it affected your choices?

3. What can you release right now?

THE SUM CHALLENGE:

Put down one emotional weight you were never meant to carry.

PRAYER FOR THE JOURNEY:

God, show me what I no longer need and give me peace as I release it. Amen.

"You cannot outlead the wounds you refuse to confront."

CHAPTER 3

THE SHAPING OF A LEADER YOU DO NOT SEE

There comes a moment in every person's life when you realize that the version of yourself you show to the world is not the one you carry in silence. You may appear steady, capable, or even confident, yet underneath are experiences that shaped you long before you had the language to explain them. Before you read further, pause and ask yourself a simple question: What did you survive that shaped you long before anyone knew who you were?

The depth of your answer reveals more about your leadership than any title ever will.

Leadership begins in the hidden places. It begins in the days when no one is applauding you, when circumstances force you to stretch, and when you learn more about yourself than you want anyone else to know. Before leadership becomes visible, it is formed in the quiet shaping of your mindset, your resilience, and your identity.

THE WEIGHT YOU LEARN TO CARRY ALONE

When I left home at sixteen, I believed distance would fix what confusion and hurt had broken inside me. I carried anger that felt normal, not because I enjoyed it, but because I didn't know what else to feel. I carried confusion about my past, the kind you learn to bury because there is no safe place to unpack it. I carried the pressure of becoming someone strong, even though I felt anything but strong.

That weight did not disappear when I stepped off the Greyhound bus in Ypsilanti, Michigan. Instead, it followed me into a new environment where I was forced to grow up faster than I realized. I was a kid trying to blend in while holding myself together with whatever scraps of dignity I could find.

That is the first truth of becoming. Changing your environment does not change your internal world. You carry your unhealed story with you until you decide to SEE it.

THE HIDDEN STRUGGLE AT SCHOOL

Despite everything happening outside of school, I still showed up. Not because I was dedicated, but because school was the one place where I could sit down without worrying about where I would sleep that night. It was the only place where exhaustion felt normal.

I slept in class because the streets didn't offer real rest. Teachers scolded me, thinking I was disrespectful or lazy, never realizing that sleep was survival. I ate when I could, and on days when money was scarce, I played tonk with cards on the top of tables, trash cans, or whatever surface I could find between classes, hoping to win enough for a honey bun and jungle juice. People saw a kid hustling. They didn't see a kid hungry.

My sweatshirt said "Lincoln Volleyball," even though I had never played volleyball in my life. I found it in a locker room closet, left behind by someone who didn't need it. To me, it felt like protection. It was the closest thing I had to belonging. It gave me a chance to blend in, even if only for a day or two at a time.

Most days, I walked the halls trying to keep my head down. I didn't want questions. I didn't want sympathy. I didn't want to be seen as the kid who couldn't survive on his own. I was fighting battles that no one around me recognized.

When people only see your behavior, they misinterpret your reality. Leadership requires the ability to SEE beneath the surface... starting with yourself.

THE SOCIAL WORKER WHO SAW THROUGH THE MASK

The school social worker called me into her office nearly every day I was in school. She always asked the same question: "Are you okay?"

I always gave the same answer: "I'm fine."

She saw the fatigue in my eyes, the restlessness in my behavior, the signs that something was wrong. At sixteen, I didn't have the words to explain what survival felt like. Emotional numbness becomes a skill when pain has nowhere to go. Acting unbothered becomes a shield. Silence becomes a strategy.

She kept checking in. I kept pretending I didn't need help. Looking back, I realize she saw through the mask I fought to hold in place. She just didn't yet have permission to reach behind it.

Sometimes leadership begins with being seen by someone who refuses to stop asking.

THE FIGHTS THAT WERE NEVER ABOUT THE FIGHTS

During that season, I got into fights because anger was the only currency I understood at the time. I was frustrated, tired, and overwhelmed. Every small wrong felt like an attack. Every disagreement felt like disrespect. When you are hurting, everything looks like a threat.

People saw the behavior. They didn't see the boy underneath who was drowning in silence.

Anger is often the language of the unheard. It becomes the expression of pain that hasn't been processed. If no one teaches you how to articulate hurt, you learn to express it with volume or violence. That was me at sixteen.

Hurt that is not UNDERSTOOD will always find expression somewhere.

THE MOMENT OF INTERVENTION

The turning point did not happen because I suddenly had clarity. It happened because someone intervened when I no longer knew how to ask for help.

The judge who reviewed my case saw the reality behind the behavior. My parents saw what isolation and instability were doing to me. Together, they pulled me out of the environment I believed I had to endure. They brought me home, because they saw what I could not see.

I thought independence meant managing everything alone. They knew independence, at that age, was slowly destroying me.

That intervention did more than change my circumstances. It forced me to confront a truth I had avoided. Strength is not the absence of struggle. Strength is knowing when you are not okay and allowing someone to help you rebuild.

Intervention is often the first stop toward UNDERSTANDING your own story.

THE REAL BEGINNING OF LEADERSHIP

It took time to understand what that season taught me. Leadership did not begin with authority, it began with recognition. I learned that:

people often carry burdens in silence

behavior is a language

anger usually hides hurt

pride can block healing

leadership requires empathy above all else

identity forms in the moments that feel unfair

Those months shaped the way I would one day lead teams, influence Soldiers, develop young leaders, and support people who didn't have the words to describe what they were fighting.

You cannot lead people well if you only see their actions. You must understand their story.

Leaders grow when they learn to UNDERSTAND people, not judge them.

THE SUM OF YOUR BECOMING

This is where the concept of Black Leadership becomes real. The color black absorbs all light. In the same way, leadership absorbs every part of your experience. Your hardships. Your strengths. Your insecurities. Your breakthroughs. Your unspoken battles. Your unseen victories.

Leadership is the sum of everything that has shaped you, not just the parts you are proud of.

The version of me that returned home after Michigan was different. Not wiser or stronger yet, but more aware. I understood that the world tests you long before it teaches you. I understood that people judge what they cannot see. And I understood that survival was never meant to be the destination.

Leaders are not defined by how well they perform in public. They are defined by how honestly they confront who they are in private.

This chapter is about that beginning.

The quiet, unglamorous forming of character.

The part of your story that becomes the foundation for everything that follows.

Your becoming starts in the places no one applauds.

This is the part of leadership where you begin to MANIFEST who you are becoming, not who you were trying to survive as.

Chapter 3 SUM IT UP

THE SUM FRAMEWORK: SEE + UNDERSTAND + MANIFEST

Your unseen years shaped you more than any applause ever could.

SEE: the quiet seasons that built your character.

UNDERSTAND: the lessons you gained in silence.

MANIFEST: truth by leading from who you really are.

BECOMING THE SUM:

1. What silent season taught you the most?

2. What lesson from that time still guides you?

3. How can you walk in that truth today?

THE SUM CHALLENGE:

Acknowledge one lesson from your past with gratitude.

PRAYER FOR THE JOURNEY:

God, remind me of the value in every season and help me lead with wisdom. Amen.

"The loudest battles are the ones no one sees."

CHAPTER 4

THE TURNING POINT OF BECOMING

There are seasons in life when the direction of your story changes without announcement. You do not notice the shift at first. You only feel something stirring inside you, something that refuses to let you live the way you used to. These moments often arrive quietly, long before you understand how significant they will become. What you choose in these moments begins shaping the person you are becoming.

My shift began the day I entered the United States Army. The first thing that struck me was the noise. Running boots and shouted instructions. Metal doors slamming. Commands echoing through hallways. The energy of a place where hesitation had no place. It was a sudden contrast to what I had known. For the first time, I stepped into a world where structure outweighed survival.

The Army did not allow you to hide behind emotion. It did not adjust itself to your story. It did not pause to see if you were comfortable. It forced you to meet a level of discipline that revealed the gaps inside you. For someone who had survived chaos and learned to depend on himself, this was unfamiliar, but it gave me something I needed. Predictability. Expectations. Order.

But stability does not automatically create growth. It exposes the parts of you you have been avoiding. And the Army exposed mine quickly.

It was here that the early seeds of SUM began forming long before I ever had language for them. These moments taught me to SEE myself honestly, UNDERSTAND where discipline was missing, and begin MANIFESTING a different version of myself one decision at a time.

EARLY HUMBLING AND EARLY LESSONS

I remember being corrected in front of the platoon for reacting slowly to instruction. Nothing dramatic, but enough to remind me that effort alone would not carry me. That moment was small, but it sat with me for the rest of the day. I learned endurance was not the same as discipline. I had spent years believing that endurance was strength. But endurance only takes you so far. What I lacked was discipline. Consistency. Awareness.

One of my drill sergeants noticed something in me early on. He saw the way I responded when corrected. He pushed me harder. Not with kindness, but with intention. He understood the difference between a young man acting out of arrogance and a young man acting out of pain. He did not allow me to retreat into excuses, and he did not allow emotion to dictate my performance.

He told me something I never forgot.

"You can win here, but not with the habits that brought you here."

It was the simplest way anyone had ever explained growth to me.

That sentence became one of the first moments I truly SEE myself. It revealed what needed to change and gave me the awareness to UNDERSTAND my own patterns. It taught me that the life I wanted would require a new level of discipline I needed to MANIFEST day after day.

THE MOMENT THAT REVEALED THE LEADER I WANTED TO BE

One of the most defining experiences of that period had nothing to do with discipline drills or physical training. It happened in the bay, during a night that changed the way I understood leadership.

There was a trainee in our platoon who had been a state champion in cross country. His endurance was unmatched, but he struggled with certain motor skills and had a speech pattern that made him a target that people picked on. In an environment designed to break you down, he stood out. And instead of supporting him, some of the other trainees made him a target for their frustration.

One night, they threw his sneakers into the dumpster behind the barracks. It was late, and the only light we had came from a dim security lamp and the red glow of our headlamps. I remember the look on his face when he realized they were gone. Confusion. Embarrassment. A kind of hurt I recognized from my own life. It reminded me of moments when people mistook my silence for weakness and my struggle for indifference.

We walked behind the building and began searching through trash bags, shifting through old food and empty boxes, our breath visible in the night air. I remember the cold metal of the dumpster against my hands as I climbed inside to help him. We finally found the shoes at the bottom, soaked and dirty. He said thank you quietly, barely loud enough to hear.

But the incident that followed was worse.

During mail call the next evening, one of the drill sergeants mocked him. Mimicked his voice. Laughed at his struggle. The entire bay fell silent. It was the kind of silence that holds both fear and helplessness. Everyone looked down. No one spoke.

My heart was pounding in my chest. I was afraid. I needed the Army. I needed the opportunity. I could not afford to make a mistake. But I also could not stand there and watch someone be humiliated, not after everything I had lived through. Not after everything I had survived in silence.

I stepped forward and said, "Drill Sergeant, that is not right."

The room still silent.

He ordered everyone else out. The bay emptied in seconds, boots pounding the floor as the platoon vanished into the hallway. Then he turned to me.

For the next hour, he smoked me until sweat covered the floor. My arms shook. My chest burned. My legs tightened. Every muscle screamed. But I did not quit. I stayed respectful. I stayed present. I absorbed every second because I knew I had made the right choice.

When he finally stopped, he said nothing. He walked out of the bay and shut the door behind him.

The mocking stopped.

The teasing stopped.

The platoon noticed.

That night, I understood something about myself that I had never seen clearly before. Leadership was not about rank or authority. It was about courage. It was about character. It was about being the voice you once needed.

What happened in that bay did more than test my courage. It showed me the kind of leader I was becoming. Not perfect or polished. But willing. And willingness is often the first manifestation of leadership before skills ever catch up.

As training continued, I began to see the difference between doing enough and becoming enough. Mediocrity no longer felt like an option because I had lived too many years fighting. Now that I was in an environment where excellence was possible, I wanted to rise into it.

Discipline slowly replaced defensiveness.

Consistency replaced emotion.

Purpose replaced insecurity.

I started waking up with a deeper intention. I wanted to be someone others could rely on. Someone who did what was right instead of what was easy. Someone who spoke up when others stayed silent. Someone who could be counted on when things went wrong.

Leadership was taking root inside me, not through authority, but through the choices I made when no one was commanding me to make them.

This was the earliest formation of identity-driven leadership. I was learning to SEE who I wanted to be, UNDERSTAND what it required, and MANIFEST the habits that would turn potential into reality.

THE FIRST WHISPERS OF A BIGGER CALLING

By the time my initial training period ended, I could feel the shift happening inside me. The Army had become a mirror, showing me both my potential and my weaknesses. And in that reflection, a new desire began forming.

I started watching Soldiers from elite units. They carried themselves differently. They moved with purpose. Their discipline was evident long before they spoke. Their presence alone commanded respect. They were not loud. They were not arrogant. They were simply exceptional.

I did not fully understand their world yet. But I knew I wanted to reach for something greater than what I had settled for in the past. Something that required more of me than survival. Something that required a higher standard.

The path to Ranger Regiment began as a whisper inside me long before I ever committed to it. It was the recognition that there was more in me, and if I did not pursue it, I would regret it.

This chapter of my life marked the turning point. The moment I shifted from reacting to life to becoming intentional with it. The moment I began transforming from someone shaped by circumstances into someone shaped by purpose.

I did not become a leader in a day.

But in these days, I began to understand the leader I was meant to become.

That whisper was not ambition. It was alignment.

Growth does not come from the moments where you feel strong. Growth comes from the moments where you choose integrity over approval. Where you choose character over convenience. Where you choose responsibility over fear.

Those decisions quietly form the foundation of the leader you become. Everything in this chapter was part of a larger process. The discipline, the structure, the early humbling, the courage to stand up for someone else, the whispers of a higher calling, all of it was preparing me for the road ahead. None of these experiences made sense at the time, but they became essential pieces of the leader I would one day need to be. That is the truth about transformation.

You are not shaped by single events.

You are shaped by the accumulation of them.

The ones that break you.

The ones that build you.

The ones that teach you.

The ones that reveal you.

The ones that challenge the parts of you you thought were permanent.

Leadership is not formed by one defining moment. Leadership is the sum of every moment that demands you decide who you are becoming.

Just as the color black absorbs all light, you absorb every lesson life hands you. Every choice. Every hardship. Every breakthrough. Every act of courage. Every moment of clarity. They all become part of the leader emerging within you.

You are becoming the sum of your experiences, your values, your courage, and your calling.

Chapter 4 SUM IT UP

THE SUM FRAMEWORK: SEE + UNDERSTAND + MANIFEST

Healing starts when you stop running from what hurt you.

SEE: the pain you pushed down.

UNDERSTAND: how it shaped your reactions and trust.

MANIFEST: healing by naming what needs attention.

BECOMING THE SUM:

1. What old pain still speaks in your life?

2. How did it shape your choices?

3. What step toward healing can you take today?

THE SUM CHALLENGE:

Write down the wound you are ready to face.

PRAYER FOR THE JOURNEY:

God, help me face what hurt me and guide me into real healing. Amen.

"Healing begins the moment you stop waiting to be rescued."

CHAPTER 5

THE ROAD THAT CALLS YOU

FORWARD

There are seasons in life when everything around you looks familiar, yet something is off or feels different. You might wake up in the same home, drive the same route, and interact with the same people, but a quiet tension grows inside you that suggests you cannot remain who you have always been. This tension is not loud or dramatic. It starts as a subtle sense that the patterns you have mastered no longer match the person you are becoming. It is the first sign that purpose is rising inside you.

This internal pull is universal. A student may sense they were meant for more than simply attending classes and turning in assignments. A teacher may feel a desire to impact lives on a deeper level than the system allows. A corporate professional may sense a calling to step away from comfort and into purpose, even if the next steps are unclear. An entrepreneur may feel an idea persist in their mind long after they have tried to dismiss it. A leader may realize that their influence requires growth beyond a title or position. Regardless of your role or stage of life, there comes a moment when something inside you begins to push against the boundaries you once accepted.

Comfort is one of the most deceptive places a person can live. It presents itself as stability, but underneath it often hides stagnation. People remain in comfortable environments because comfort gives them just enough progress to avoid confronting their potential. Students settle for doing the minimum required to get by, even when they are capable of far more. Professionals show up consistently but rarely stretch their abilities. Leaders manage instead of inspiring because managing feels safer. Entrepreneurs abandon ideas because fear convinces them that stability matters more than vision. Parents maintain patterns that feel familiar even when those patterns do not serve the family they want to build.

I found myself in a similar place. I had become comfortable in my role, in my routines, and in my daily responsibilities. I understood the expectations placed on me, and I knew how to meet them. Yet comfort did not challenge me. It did not stretch me or demand anything new from me. Eventually I realized the version of myself that comfort protected could not grow into the version of myself that purpose required.

Purpose is shaped in the places where you must stretch, risk, and trust.

Every environment reveals examples of excellence if you are willing to look closely. In the military, I saw Soldiers whose discipline was woven into the smallest details of their day. Their posture, focus, and consistency made it clear that they lived with intention. They did not simply perform well. They embodied excellence.

You see the same thing in civilian life. There are teachers who prepare for their students as if each day might alter the course of a child's life. There are young professionals who go beyond assigned tasks because they understand excellence attracts opportunity. There are parents who show up with intentionality because they refuse to repeat the patterns of their past. There are entrepreneurs who treat their dreams as responsibilities, not hobbies.

Excellence exists everywhere. When you witness it, something begins to awaken in you and forces you to SEE yourself differently.

The shift toward purpose always brings an internal conflict. No matter how skilled or experienced a person becomes, they will always battle two voices. One voice tells you that you are capable of more. The other voice tells you that you are not ready, not qualified, or not worthy of rising higher.

This tension exists in students, in teachers, in corporate leaders, in young professionals, and in entrepreneurs. It exists in parents who want to raise their children differently than they were raised. It exists in leaders who have grown accustomed to familiar patterns. It exists in anyone standing between who they were and who they are becoming. This conflict is a sign of awakening, not fear. It is a sign that you are crossing into a higher dimension of your identity. It is the moment where you begin to UNDERSTAND that growth is calling you forward.

My own decision to pursue a more demanding path did not come from ambition or pride. It came from the realization that staying where I was would not help me grow. I needed to pursue a place that demanded the best of me. I needed an environment where discipline was not optional. I needed challenges that would reveal my weaknesses and force them to become strengths. Many people face similar decisions in their own lives.

A teacher might lead a new program even when it feels intimidating. A professional might pursue a degree or certification that will elevate their career. A parent might choose healing so they can build a different future for their children. A leader might take full responsibility for a team instead of avoiding the weight of their influence. An employee might pursue advancement not for recognition but for purpose.

Growth requires intention, and intention requires leaving behind the environments that no longer stretch you.

When you step toward your next level, something begins to change within you. You start to show up differently. You wake with more clarity. You think with more intention. You begin to take ownership of your habits, your discipline, and your future. These shifts are often subtle. They happen when no one is watching, in the small decisions you make each day. This is the beginning of becoming someone capable of MANIFESTING purpose.

You may begin studying harder, preparing more thoroughly, or managing your time with greater care. You may start seeking guidance from people you respect or distancing yourself from relationships that no longer support your growth. These small internal victories matter. They lay the foundation for everything that comes next.

Growth often feels invisible before it becomes undeniable.

Over time, the person you once were begins to fade as new habits, new thinking, and new clarity take shape. You begin to recognize that you can no longer accept the version of yourself that once felt normal. You start to see possibilities where you once saw limitations. You become more willing to confront the areas of your life that need to change. You begin to hold yourself accountable in ways you did not before.

This is where purpose starts to reveal itself. Purpose does not arrive suddenly. It unfolds through consistency and courage.

As you move forward, it is important to reflect on what is rising within you. Consider which parts of your life feel too small for who you are becoming. Reflect on where you have chosen comfort instead of growth. Ask yourself what fear has prevented you from taking your next step. Identify the internal voice you have listened to for too long. And consider what opportunities you have postponed because you doubted your readiness. These questions are not meant to shame you. They are meant to illuminate the areas where transformation is waiting.

Everything you have lived through is preparing you for everything you are called to become. Greatness is not a single moment. It is the result of accumulated decisions, lessons, and experiences that shape you over time. Just as the color black absorbs all light, your becoming absorbs every experience. Every challenge, every moment of clarity, every internal battle, and every small victory contributes to the sum of who you are.

You are not reading this chapter by coincidence. You are in a season of preparation. You are being shaped for something greater than the role you currently occupy.

The road that calls you forward is not asking you to be perfect. It is asking you to be willing. When you choose willingness, you choose transformation. And transformation is the beginning of purpose.

Everything you have lived through is preparing you for everything you are called to become. Greatness is not a single moment. It is the sum of every decision, every lesson, every challenge, and every rising.

Just as the color black absorbs all light, your becoming absorbs every experience.

Every struggle.

Every victory.

Every correction.

Every rising.

You are being prepared for something greater than where you are now.

Chapter 5 SUM IT UP

THE SUM FRAMEWORK: SEE + UNDERSTAND + MANIFEST

Your identity becomes stronger when you confront the lies that tried to define you.

SEE: the false beliefs you accepted.

UNDERSTAND: how those beliefs limited your confidence.

MANIFEST: truth by embracing who God says you are.

BECOMING THE SUM:

1. What lie shaped your identity?

2. How did it influence your behavior?

3. What truth are you ready to live out?

THE SUM CHALLENGE:

Replace one false belief with a true one.

PRAYER FOR THE JOURNEY:

God, replace every lie in me with truth and restore my identity. Amen.

"Your truth is not weakness, it is your turning point."

CHAPTER 6

ENTERING THE WORLD OF EXCELLENCE

There are environments in life that do not simply change you. They reveal you. They confront the identity you brought with you and require you to become someone new if you plan to remain. For me, Ranger Regiment was one of those places. It was more than a unit or a job. It was a world built on a standard that very few ever experience. Stepping into it felt like stepping into a different dimension, one where comfort had no place and potential was measured through discipline, precision, and the willingness to grow daily.

Before I arrived, I carried the pride of having made it through selection. I had endured long nights, relentless rucks, exhaustion layered on exhaustion, and the mental battles that unfold when quitting begins to whisper as a viable option. But what I did not know at the time was that selection was simply the doorframe. The real test began when I walked through it.

The first thing I noticed about Regiment was the pace. Everything moved fast. People moved with purpose. No one wandered or hesitated. The smallest habits carried meaning, and the details others might ignore were the very things that defined success or failure. The tempo alone was enough to reveal whether you were prepared or merely hoping to blend in. In most places, confidence can hide in the shadows of mediocrity. In elite environments, confidence is exposed by your performance.

I entered this world not as someone following a well-worn path, but as the first person in my field to ever be accepted into it. I did not understand the historical significance then. I was not thinking about becoming the first geospatial engineer in Regiment history. I was still trying to outrun the parts of me that felt stuck. I wanted to serve at a higher level, not for recognition or a legacy, but because something in me needed to rise. Being first came with a pressure I could not name at the time. There was no blueprint for how to do this job in this environment. There was only expectation. The standard of Regiment did not shift to accommodate what I did not know. I had to elevate to match what the organization required.

Early on, the culture revealed itself through silence more than through instruction. No one had to announce the standard. You could feel it in the way Rangers moved, spoke, trained, and executed. Excellence was not something talked about. It was something lived without exception. If you failed, you learned quickly. If you succeeded, you continued without celebration. In this world, you were never as good as your last performance. You were only as good as your next one.

It did not take long for me to realize that being part of Regiment meant carrying an immense responsibility. Mistakes had consequences beyond embarrassment. They carried weight that affected teams, missions, and lives. Precision was not optional. Readiness was not a slogan. It was a way of existing. That understanding reshaped me. It made me accountable for the smallest details of my actions and my thinking. I grew more in the first several months in Regiment than I had in years because the environment demanded it.

This experience may sound distant from civilian life at first glance, but the truth is that every high-performing environment carries its own version of these moments. A teacher stepping into a school with a culture of excellence must elevate the way they prepare and engage. A young professional entering a competitive field learns quickly that effort must be matched with precision. A parent raising children with intention must operate at a level of discipline and emotional resilience that does not allow complacency. An entrepreneur trying to build something meaningful must adapt to a pace and demand that challenge their old habits. A leader attempting to influence a team must model the standard they expect from others.

Whether you enter a boardroom, a classroom, a studio, a courthouse, a hospital, or a business you are building from the ground up, the environments that stretch you are not that different from the one I entered. Excellence has a language that transcends fields. It is spoken through preparation, ownership, discipline, and consistency.

As I settled into Regiment, the early days felt like a constant test. Every task mattered. Even small responsibilities carried significance. You could not hide behind effort alone. Performance had to match intent. I had to learn the job from the inside out, translate my skills into a setting that demanded speed and accuracy, and understand how to contribute meaningfully to a team where every role played into the success of the mission. At times, I felt out of place. I questioned whether I belonged among men who had cultivated excellence long before I arrived.

That internal conflict taught me my first true leadership lesson inside Regiment:

Belonging is not something you wait to feel. It is something you build through consistency.

I began to SEE myself honestly, UNDERSTAND the gaps that still needed refinement, and MANIFEST the habits that matched the environment I had stepped into.

The more I leaned in, the more I recognized that excellence is not a talent. It is a habit shaped by the environment you choose and the standards you accept. The people around me became mirrors. Their discipline reflected what I lacked. Their precision revealed where I needed to mature. Their commitment showed me what it truly meant to serve. This is why environments matter. You cannot become extraordinary in a place that allows you to remain average. You must place yourself where excellence is the baseline and growth is the expectation.

Civilians experience this same truth. A student's potential expands when surrounded by classmates who push themselves academically. A corporate employee rises when working among people who expect innovation and responsibility. A teacher grows when working beside colleagues who refuse to lower the bar. An entrepreneur accelerates when surrounded by others building at a high level. The environment you choose shapes the leader you become.

As the months passed, Regiment began to change me. I started thinking differently. I began anticipating needs instead of waiting for direction. I paid attention to detail in ways I never had before. I understood the value of preparation and the necessity of adaptability. I realized that my presence contributed to the team, not because of my title or my skill set, but because I showed up each day ready to grow.

One night, while preparing for an operation, I triple-checked a piece of my equipment that I had inspected earlier that day. Something felt off. The straps on my kit had loosened. A detail easy to overlook. Fixing it took less than a minute. Ignoring it could have cost us hours. No one saw it. No one praised it. But in that moment, I understood what Regiment was teaching me. Excellence is not what you do when people are watching. Excellence is what you refuse to overlook when no one will ever know.

Regiment revealed something essential. High-performing environments do not transform you by accident. They transform you because they force you to confront yourself. You learn where you are undisciplined, where you lack clarity, where you operate from fear, and where you avoid responsibility. Growth begins the moment you stop resisting the lessons these environments teach.

This truth applies in every corner of life. The teacher who chooses to innovate rather than complain begins to transform. The young professional who seeks mentorship instead of avoiding feedback matures faster. The entrepreneur who embraces discomfort learns to build with resilience. The leader who takes responsibility for their influence becomes someone others want to follow. Transformation begins not through comfort but through confrontation.

Regiment taught me that purpose is not revealed in one moment. It unfolds through repetition. It grows through discipline. It sharpens through pressure. It deepens through service. It becomes visible over time as you embrace the environments and experiences that shape you.

By the end of my first year, I understood that I was not there merely to excel at a job. I was there to become someone worthy of the opportunities ahead. I began to see how every task, every responsibility, and every challenge was forming a version of me that I did not know existed when I first arrived. That realization carried weight.

Your own journey may look different, but the principle remains the same. You are becoming someone new in the presence of the environments that demand your growth. The question is not whether life is shaping you. The question is whether you will allow the shaping to be intentional.

As you reflect on your story, consider where excellence is calling you to rise. Think about the environments that stretch you and the habits they are shaping. Ask yourself what version of yourself you need to let go of and what version you need to step into. Just like Ranger Regiment sharpened me, your environment is sharpening you. The purpose that awaits you is the sum of every experience, every lesson, and every stretch that brings you closer to who you were meant to become.

You are not meant to remain the same.

You are meant to rise.

Chapter 6 SUM IT UP

THE SUM FRAMEWORK: SEE + UNDERSTAND + MANIFEST

Life repeats what you avoid. Growth happens when you pay attention.

SEE: the patterns you fall into.

UNDERSTAND: what those patterns reveal.

MANIFEST: alignment by choosing differently.

BECOMING THE SUM:

1. What pattern keeps showing up?

2. What truth is behind it?

3. What aligned choice can you make today?

THE SUM CHALLENGE:

Interrupt one old pattern with a different action.

PRAYER FOR THE JOURNEY:

God, show me what needs to change and help me walk in alignment. Amen.

"Excellence is built in the shadows before it is revealed in the light."

CHAPTER 7

THE WEIGHT THAT SHAPES YOU

Responsibility has a way of maturing you long before you feel ready for it. In Ranger Regiment, responsibility was not a concept written in doctrine or spoken in long speeches. It was something you carried in your chest, something you felt in the silence, something that became heavier with every name you lost. It began as pressure, the kind that comes with a demanding environment and high expectations. Over time, that pressure transformed into something deeper, something that reached into your identity and reshaped how you saw yourself in the world.

In the early years, I believed responsibility was simply about doing my job well, protecting standards, and contributing to the mission. But responsibility changes when you begin to lose the people you serve beside. The first time it happened, the weight of it sank into me in a way I could not articulate. I lost friends in combat, men whose laughter I still hear sometimes in quiet moments. Some died from natural causes far earlier than they should have. And the losses that pierced the deepest were those who took their own lives. Brothers who still had potential, purpose, and an entire world left to give, yet somehow slipped beyond the reach of the very brotherhood that had held them through the hardest moments of war.

There is a pain that settles into you when someone who once stood in the same formation, walked the same dirt, and faced the same darkness decides that their story has reached its end. It is not the kind of pain that flares up all at once. It settles slowly, like a shadow that stretches wider with time. I looked at their lives and felt a truth I could not escape. If they could not finish living their dream, then I owed them the responsibility of living mine with more intention.

It was not survivor's guilt as much as it was survivor's responsibility. I felt obligated to build the life that so many of them deserved but never got the chance to see. Every time I received bad news, something in me hardened and softened at the same time. Hardened in resolve. Softened in empathy. Their lives, their struggles, and their unfinished stories forced me to look at my own reflection with a level of honesty I had never carried before.

This was the beginning of my rise. It did not come from ambition or a desire to be the best. It came from grief that demanded purpose. I became relentless, not because I wanted accolades, but because I refused to waste the breath that my brothers no longer had.

It was the moment I began to SEE the weight inside me with new clarity. The moment grief pushed me to UNDERSTAND the excellence without healing would never be enough. And the moment purpose began to MANIFEST through responsibility that felt sacred.

Responsibility became personal. It became sacred. And slowly, it became transformational.

As the years progressed, my performance reflected the intensity of that transformation. For well over a decade, I found myself ranking at the very top of every promotion list. I became number one on every order of merit list. I graduated every course within the top ten percent. My professional evaluations consistently reflected the highest marks. And, almost ironically, I maintained a perfect 4.0 GPA through academic pursuits that would have overwhelmed me years earlier.

But excellence does not erase pain. It organizes it. It channels it. It directs it toward something meaningful.

I was not rising because life had become easy. I was rising because life had become heavy, and rising was the only way to carry the weight without collapsing.

Yet even as my professional life ascended, my personal life reflected the part of me that was still trying to heal. I experienced three divorces. Each one exposed wounds I had not fully understood. I was still carrying grief that had not been processed, loss that had not been acknowledged, and pain that had not been named. I did not yet understand that trauma does not disappear when you achieve. It hides beneath performance until you are ready to confront it.

From the outside, it looked as if I was excelling. On the inside, I was trying to figure out how to be whole. But growth often works like this. You mature in one dimension while healing in another. You succeed in one area while struggling in a different one. You learn how to lead teams long before you learn how to lead your own heart. Responsibility in one area does not exempt you from brokenness in another. It simply forces you to face it eventually.

The turning point arrived when I realized that responsibility was not something I carried for my teams alone. It was something I needed to carry for myself. The grief that drove my excellence was real, but excellence could not heal the parts of me I had avoided. That healing began with a moment I did not expect. I had been in therapy for years, but something inside me always held back. I learned how to survive, how to function, how to stay afloat. But I had not learned how to confront the deeper layers of myself.

Then, one day, I found myself in a room with a coach. It felt different from therapy. The moment the session began, something inside me softened in a way I had never experienced. I melted. Years of suppressed emotion surfaced. The pain I had carried for so long finally had space to breathe. Yet alongside the tears came questions that forced introspection. Questions that did not allow me to hide behind strength or performance. Questions that pushed me to consider not only who I had become, but who I wanted to be.

That session changed my life. It introduced me to a level of self-leadership that I had never encountered before. And in 2018, I began the journey to become a professional coach. I had no idea then that I would become the first enlisted active duty executive coach in the Special Operations community and the first in the entire Department of Defense. I joined a cohort filled with officers, senior civilians, doctors, psychologists, and lawyers. Yet none of those differences mattered in that room. What connected us was pain, growth, and the shared hunger to become better versions of ourselves.

My coaching journey did not begin from a desire to achieve another milestone. It began because healing had finally taught me that leadership must include the emotional, relational, and spiritual dimensions of a person. I learned that people rise not only through discipline or excellence, but through introspection, vulnerability, and empathy. Those lessons began to shape the way I coached, the way I led, and the way I lived.

Looking back, the responsibility that once felt like a burden became the very thing that refined me. The losses pushed me into purpose. The grief taught me empathy. The pressure produced excellence. The pain revealed the parts of me that needed healing. And the healing led me toward a calling that extended far beyond the uniform.

Responsibility grew because life required it. And that responsibility became the foundation that shaped my leadership more than any school, rank, or position ever could.

It was the moment responsibility evolved into identity. The moment I realized leadership is not a role you perform. It is a life you live.

In the next chapter, the path of excellence takes shape in a new way. Not through pressure alone, but through intention, discipline, and the desire to transform everything and everyone entrusted to you.

As you consider your own journey, pause for a moment and reflect on what responsibility has been trying to teach you. What weight in your life is shaping you rather than breaking you? What experiences have demanded more maturity, more intention, or more growth than you expected? And what losses or disappointments have quietly reshaped your values, your direction, or your identity? Every person carries something that forces them to rise. The question is whether you will allow it to mature you into who you are meant to become.

Every chapter of your life has contributed something to you. Every challenge has handed you a lesson. Every failure has revealed a truth. Every moment of pressure has helped define your purpose. You are not simply the product of your achievements or your resilience or your pain. You are the sum of everything you have walked through, survived, learned, and risen from.

This is the essence of Black Leadership. It is the absorption of all experiences. It is the convergence of every lesson. It is the transformation of every wound into wisdom. It is the willingness to take responsibility, even when responsibility feels heavy. It is the courage to become the sum of your journey.

Your rise continues.

Chapter 7 SUM IT UP

THE SUM FRAMEWORK: SEE + UNDERSTAND + MANIFEST

Your voice rises the moment you decide to stop shrinking.

SEE: where you have been silent.

UNDERSTAND: how silence cost you clarity.

MANIFEST: courage by speaking truth.

BECOMING THE SUM:

1. Where have you held back your voice?

2. What truth needs to be spoken?

3. What bold step can you take?

THE SUM CHALLENGE:

Say what needs to be said.

PRAYER FOR THE JOURNEY:

God, give me courage to speak clearly and confidently. Amen.

"Discipline is an agreement with your future self."

CHAPTER 8

THE ARCHITECTURE OF EXCELLENCE

Excellence is often misunderstood as something people chase for recognition, achievement, or ambition. For me, it became the natural progression of maturity. Responsibility had reshaped the way I showed up, and the environments I entered demanded a level of consistency that would stretch me into someone I had not yet become. By the time I reached the next phase of my career, I understood that excellence was no longer a response to pain. It was the discipline required to carry purpose.

Regiment had taught me to think quickly, prepare thoroughly, and stay composed under pressure. The next chapter of my journey required something more. It required precision. It required mastery. It required the ability not only to meet a standard but to anticipate the moments where the standard would be tested. The operational tempo was still intense, and the expectations were unyielding, but what changed was my approach to them. Instead of reacting to challenges as they came, I began architecting the way I performed.

Excellence became a habit long before it became a reputation. It showed up in the early mornings when I reviewed the same material others skimmed through. It showed up at night when I studied, retrained, or rewrote, or recreated products even when the first version was good enough. It showed up in the way I paid attention to details that once felt insignificant. I learned that the smallest adjustments often created the largest outcomes. Precision is rarely glamorous, but it is always powerful.

As I entered the Joint Special Operations environment, these habits began to compound. This world was not impressed by talent. It was shaped by consistency. Every person in the room carried a high level of skill, education, and experience. The difference between good and great was not the work you did when people watched, but the discipline you practiced when the room was empty. I discovered that my ability to excel was not tied to my background, my path, or even my natural abilities. It was tied to the decisions I made when no one was keeping score.

This realization built the foundation for the professional streak that marked the next decade of my career. Whether it was evaluations, promotion lists, or academic programs, I remained at the top not because I chased the position, but because I committed to the process. The process made excellence predictable. Predictability made leadership possible. Leadership made impact inevitable.

Yet excellence is not about outperforming others. It is about elevating the environment you are part of. As I grew, my teams grew. I noticed that when a leader works with intention, clarity, and discipline, the team rises without the leader needing to force anything. People respond to what they observe more than what they are told. They begin to carry themselves differently. They make decisions with more awareness. They develop a deeper respect for the work and for each other.

This is true in any field. Students elevate when the expectations around them rise. Employees flourish when leaders model consistency. Athletes improve when the team culture reinforces discipline. Families grow when one person chooses maturity. Excellence is not a private accomplishment. It is a shared transformation. The impact spreads through the culture, the relationships, and the results of the entire group.

What surprised me most during this season was how excellence began shaping my identity. At first, I had simply wanted to improve. Eventually, I wanted to contribute. Over time, I wanted to lead. I started recognizing how my mindset shifted. I began thinking several steps ahead. I became more intentional with my communication. I learned to anticipate the needs of others before they expressed them. I learned to mentor through presence rather than pressure. Excellence had matured into something deeper. It was no longer about performance. It was about responsibility.

This growth did not erase the challenges of my personal life. I was still navigating internal wounds and relational patterns that I had not yet understood. But for the first time, I was aware that professional excellence alone could not make me whole. It could strengthen my discipline. It could shape my identity. It could elevate my opportunities. But it could not heal what I had not confronted. That realization would carry me into the next stage of my life, one where I would learn that leadership cannot be sustained without emotional maturity.

Yet the lessons of excellence remained valuable. They taught me that mastery is not something you find. It is something you build. They taught me that consistency creates confidence. They taught me that leadership is a reflection of character long before it is a reflection of performance.

They taught me that excellence is not a destination. It is an identity that develops slowly through intentional decisions.

Take a moment to consider your own path. Where has discipline shaped your life? Where have small habits produced meaningful change? Where have you allowed your potential to rest when it should have been strengthened? Excellence grows wherever it is watered. It grows in students who study when it would be easier to quit. It grows in professionals who continue learning long after others plateau. It grows in parents who show up with patience even on difficult days. It grows in entrepreneurs who keep building when the results are still unseen.

Your story, like mine, is full of opportunities to rise. Every experience you have carried, every discipline you have developed, and every challenge you have faced has contributed to the person you are becoming. Excellence is not something separate from your life. It is woven into every choice that shapes your identity.

You are not defined by one achievement or one hardship. You are defined by the sum of the habits, decisions, and commitments that have brought you to this moment.

Your journey forward begins with healing.

And that healing will reveal the leader you are destined to become.

Chapter 8 SUM IT UP

THE SUM FRAMEWORK: SEE + UNDERSTAND + MANIFEST

Fear can sound reasonable. Purpose reveals what is real.

SEE: where fear is guiding your decisions.

UNDERSTAND: how it limits your growth.

MANIFEST: courage through action.

BECOMING THE SUM:

1. What decision has fear influenced?
2. What truth stands behind that fear?
3. What action requires courage today?

THE SUM CHALLENGE:

Make one decision based on purpose, not fear.

PRAYER FOR THE JOURNEY:

God, give me courage to move with purpose and clarity. Amen.

"Emotional control is the quiet force behind every great leader."

CHAPTER 9

THE CALL TO HEAL

There comes a moment in every leader's life when achievement is no longer enough to quiet the restlessness inside. You can succeed publicly while struggling privately. You can rise in your career while falling in your relationships. You can excel on the outside and still carry a quiet ache that never seems to fade. So much of leadership is built on performance, and yet the greatest damage often happens in the places no performance can reach.

Many people reach this point without ever naming it. A teacher shows up for their students but collapses emotionally at home. A manager leads their team with strength but avoids conflict in their personal life. A parent provides for their family but feels disconnected from the people they love. A young professional climbs quickly but loses themselves along the way. An entrepreneur pushes forward while ignoring the exhaustion that grows beneath the excitement. The truth is simple. You cannot lead others well until you learn to lead yourself through healing.

Healing is often misunderstood. People think healing is about forgetting the past or becoming unaffected by it.

In reality, healing is about reclaiming the parts of yourself that pain has interrupted.

It is the process of no longer letting old wounds dictate your identity, your decisions, or your relationships. Healing requires honesty. It requires courage. And it requires humility. It asks you to look inward with the same intensity you often direct outward.

The difficult part is that most people delay healing because they believe they can manage their pain while managing their responsibilities. They tell themselves they are fine. They convince themselves they can outrun the impact. They bury themselves in work, in roles, in accomplishments, or in taking care of others. Yet the unhealed parts of your life always surface. They surface in the way you communicate. They surface in what triggers you. They surface in the conflicts you avoid and the ones you create. They surface in the relationships that break when you expected them to hold.

I did not understand how unhealed I was until the parts of my life that discipline could not fix began to unravel. Even as my professional performance reached new levels, my personal life reflected the wounds I had ignored. Years of unresolved grief, internal conflict, and emotional isolation created patterns I did not have the tools to break. I was excelling in some areas and crumbling in others. Healing did not begin when I achieved more. Healing began when I finally admitted I needed it.

Your story may look different, but the principle is the same. Healing does not begin when you break. It begins when you choose to stop pretending you are unbreakable. The journey toward wholeness is not a sign of weakness. It is one of the greatest displays of strength a person can demonstrate. It takes maturity to confront pain that you have avoided for years. It takes courage to explore the parts of yourself you have kept hidden. It takes intention to break patterns that have become comfortable even when they are harmful.

The first step is acknowledgment.

You cannot heal what you are determined to ignore. Consider the places in your life where you feel stuck. Think about the habits you have built to protect yourself. Reflect on the emotional reactions you cannot fully explain. Examine the relationships where you feel misunderstood or disconnected. These are breadcrumbs. They are indicators of an internal world asking for attention.

The second step is curiosity.

Instead of judging your emotions, explore them. Instead of dismissing your reactions, understand them. Pain does not appear without a cause. Patterns do not form without a purpose. Your internal world is trying to teach you something. Healing begins when you stop resisting that message.

The third step is help.

No one heals alone. Whether your support comes through counseling, coaching, a mentor, a faith leader, a trusted relationship, or a safe community, you need a space where you can unravel without being judged. Some breakthroughs do not happen until someone else asks you the question you have been too afraid to ask yourself. That was the turning point for me. Therapy kept me afloat for years, but it was coaching that finally opened the door to deeper self-awareness. In that room, I discovered parts of myself I had never confronted. Pain surfaced that I did not expect. Clarity followed in ways I could not have predicted. Healing began because honesty finally became possible.

What matters most for you is not the method, but the willingness. Healing is not a destination. It is a discipline. It requires repeated choices to pause, reflect, adjust, and grow. It asks you to stay present even when discomfort rises. It invites you to release what no longer serves you. And it challenges you to become the version of yourself you were always meant to be.

Healing also changes the way you lead. It softens your approach. It deepens your empathy. It sharpens your discernment. It strengthens your communication. It stabilizes your presence. People feel safer around leaders who have taken the time to understand themselves. You no longer react from insecurity. You no longer lead from fear. You no longer make decisions from unresolved wounds. You become someone who can see others clearly because you have finally learned to see yourself.

Take a moment now to reflect on what your life might look like if you chose healing. Consider the peace you could gain, the clarity you could rebuild, the relationships you could strengthen, and the purpose you could rediscover. Think about how healing could influence your leadership, your work, your family, and your future. The parts of your life that feel heavy may not be signs of failure. They may be invitations to grow.

Every experience you have lived, every emotion you have carried, and every wound you have endured is part of your story. Healing does not erase them. Healing transforms them. Healing allows you to integrate your past without letting it define your future. Healing gives you the emotional depth required to lead with authenticity. It teaches you that strength is not the absence of pain. Strength is the presence of wisdom.

You are not simply the sum of your achievements. You are also the sum of your healing. The more whole you become, the more clearly you SEE + UNDERSTAND + MANIFEST the leader within you.

Your journey forward begins here.

Chapter 9 SUM IT UP

THE SUM FRAMEWORK: SEE + UNDERSTAND + MANIFEST

Your future requires habits that match the person you are becoming.

SEE: the habits that reflect an old version of you.

UNDERSTAND: why you hold onto them.

MANIFEST: new habits that support your growth.

BECOMING THE SUM:

1. What habit no longer serves you?

2. Why is it hard to let go?

3. What new practice can you start today?

THE SUM CHALLENGE:

Replace one outdated habit.

PRAYER FOR THE JOURNEY:

God, help me build habits that reflect the leader I am becoming. Amen.

"Adversity reveals leaders."

CHAPTER 10

THE SHIFT WITHIN

There comes a point in every person's life when survival is no longer enough. You can push through for years, carry responsibilities no one sees, and hold your world together with strength that costs you more than anyone will ever know. But eventually, there is a moment when something inside you whispers that the way you have been living cannot carry you into the life you are meant to build. That whisper is not weakness. It is awakening.

You might feel it as exhaustion.

You might feel it as restlessness.

You might feel it as the slow unraveling of a version of yourself you have outgrown.

Either way, the shift begins quietly before it becomes powerful.

For a long time, I mistook the weight I carried for the identity I was supposed to uphold. Leadership demanded excellence. Performance demanded perfection. Responsibility demanded composure. I measured myself by how much I could handle and how well I could hide everything that hurt. Many people live this same way. They become experts at functioning. Experts at appearing strong. Experts at holding together the parts of their life that feel like they are falling apart.

But no one can live split between who they show the world and who they are inside.

Eventually, those two versions collide.

My collision happened during a season where I was rebuilding my life from the ground up. On the outside, I was still performing well. Still working hard. Still appearing in control. On the inside, I was starting over in ways that stripped me down to nothing.

The temporary house I moved into had no running water and no electricity at the time. The air inside felt colder than the air outside. I would arrive at work early every morning, long before anyone else, so I could shower and handle my personal hygiene in the empty building. No one at work knew. No one suspected anything was wrong. They saw the same commitment. The same excellence. The same reliability. But every night I went home to a silent, dark shell of a house and slept curled inside a sleeping bag on the bare wooden floor.

Some nights I slept in my truck for warmth before forcing myself to go inside. The cold would bite through the layers of clothing I wore, and my breath would hang in the air as if the room itself was exhaling. I remember lying there one night, listening to the stillness, feeling tears roll down the side of my face. Not loud tears. Not the kind that explode out of you. These were quiet tears, the kind you barely notice until you taste the salt on your lips.

I was alone, exhausted, unsure of who I was becoming, and fully aware that I could not continue living split in half. I could not keep surviving without facing myself. I could not keep achieving externally while losing structure internally.

Then came the morning that changed everything.

A moment so simple it did not seem significant, yet it marked the beginning of my transformation.

I woke up on that cold wooden floor, curled in my sleeping bag, and felt the warmth of sunlight touch my face. It was gentle, steady, and completely unexpected. For the first time in months, I felt warmth on the inside too. It was as if the sun reached past the walls of the house and into the parts of my spirit I had kept shut down. In that moment I felt God say, with clarity I could not ignore, that things would be alright. The pain would not define me. The struggle would not drown me. The rebuilding would begin now.

That is when the shift within me began.

I realized I had been waiting for life to change on its own. Waiting for circumstances to improve. Waiting for the pain to soften. Waiting for clarity to arrive. But growth does not come through waiting. Growth begins the moment you decide to lead yourself out of the place where survival stopped being enough.

That morning I made a decision that reshaped my life.

I put time limits on the thoughts that weighed me down.

Ten minutes to acknowledge the frustration.

Five minutes to feel the sadness.

Two minutes to let the fear speak its piece.

Then I stood up and kept moving.

Not because I felt strong, but because I refused to stay broken.

That is leadership at its most personal level.

It is the moment you realize you cannot continue being carried by excuses, pain, or habits that belong to a previous version of you. It is the moment responsibility becomes sacred rather than heavy. The moment you understand that leading yourself is the prerequisite to leading anyone else.

The shift within you does not happen when your life is perfect. It happens when you finally decide that you deserve to live differently. It happens when you stop negotiating with your old patterns and begin building new ones. It happens when you stop hiding your hurt and start healing it. It happens when you stop chasing external validation and start becoming rooted internally.

This chapter is about that shift.

And it belongs to you as much as it belongs to me.

You may be in your own version of a cold, dark room. It may not look like mine, but the feeling is familiar. You may be rebuilding your life after disappointment. You may be learning to forgive yourself. You may be rediscovering your identity. You may be carrying responsibility at a level no one around you understands. You may be rising from a season that tested every part of your character.

Wherever you are, the shift begins when you decide that your story is not over. It begins when you choose to rebuild your inner world with the same commitment you have given to external success. It begins when you stop settling for fragments of yourself and start becoming whole again.

So pause for a moment and turn inward.

What is your shift trying to tell you?

What truth have you been avoiding?

What part of you is asking to grow?

What version of yourself are you being called to leave behind?

Transformation begins the moment you answer these questions with honesty.

Every part of your journey has strengthened you, shaped you, challenged you, and prepared you. You are not the sum of what you have survived. **You are the sum of what you are willing to become.**

And that is the beginning of becoming the sum.

Chapter 10 SUM IT UP

THE SUM FRAMEWORK: SEE + UNDERSTAND + MANIFEST

Boundaries protect your identity and your peace.

SEE: where your boundaries are weak.

UNDERSTAND: how it affects your life.

MANIFEST: strength by enforcing what matters.

BECOMING THE SUM:

1. Where do you need stronger boundaries?

2. What drains your energy?

3. What boundary can you set today?

THE SUM CHALLENGE:

Set one clear boundary and keep it.

PRAYER FOR THE JOURNEY:

God, give me strength to protect my peace and identity. Amen.

"Character is who you are in the rooms where applause cannot reach you."

CHAPTER 11

THE DISCIPLINE OF PURPOSE

Purpose is not discovered in a single moment. It is uncovered through the slow, intentional work of becoming the person you were created to be. The shift that begins inside you will always lead you toward a new standard, but the transformation that follows will depend on the discipline you build around it. Awakening opens your eyes. Discipline changes your life.

Many people wait for purpose to arrive fully formed. They want revelation without responsibility. They want clarity without sacrifice. They want transformation without structure. But purpose is not something you stumble into.

Purpose is something you grow into.

It demands participation. It demands consistency. It demands a willingness to rise even on the days when you feel unprepared or uninspired.

When I began rebuilding my life, everything in me wanted the healing to be instant. I wanted peace without the practice it required. I wanted the results without the refinement. But no matter how much pain I carried or how deeply I wanted to change, nothing shifted until I decided to discipline myself into becoming the man I needed to be. The cold mornings on that wooden floor taught me something I had never learned before. **Pain may wake you up, but discipline keeps you moving.**

This is where purpose becomes practical. Too often, purpose is treated like an emotion or a feeling. But purpose is much more stable than emotion.

Purpose lives where discipline lives.

Purpose thrives where structure thrives. Purpose expands where commitment expands. When you begin building consistent habits around who you want to become, your purpose begins to reveal itself in the spaces you once filled with uncertainty.

During my early years in Ranger Regiment and later in the Joint Special Operations Command, discipline was not optional. It was foundational. Every movement, every decision, every repetition mattered. Standards were not suggestions. Excellence was not a preference. It was the expectation every single day. But what I learned later in life was that discipline outside of purpose becomes hollow. It may produce results, but it does not produce identity.

There came a point where I had to stop performing discipline and start living discipline. I began to ask myself deeper questions. Why do I do what I do? Why do I respond the way I respond? Why do I push myself to the edge of exhaustion? Why do I avoid certain truths? Why do I crave achievement, validation, or accomplishment? The answers were rarely simple, but they revealed the root of who I was becoming.

Purpose is not discovered by looking outward. It is revealed by looking inward. Discipline gives that inward work the structure it needs to take shape.

One practice that changed my life was setting time limits on the emotional weight I carried. It was not about suppressing what I felt. It was about managing how long I allowed certain thoughts to control my direction. The more I trained myself to process what I felt with intention, the more clarity I gained. Little by little, I learned to lead my emotions instead of being led by them. This is what it means to develop internal discipline. It is the daily work of refusing to let old patterns dictate your future.

As my discipline aligned with my healing, a new clarity emerged. I began to recognize how much responsibility I held, not just in the roles I served, but in the lives connected to mine. The deaths of friends weighed heavily on me. Some fell in combat. Some to illness. But the ones that cut the deepest were the ones who lost their fight with themselves. They were men with extraordinary potential, but their pain convinced them they no longer had purpose.

Their absence became an anchor for me. I knew I could not waste the life I still had. I could not go through the motions while they never had the chance to continue their stories. I began to elevate everything in my life, not out of ambition, but out of honor. Their memory drove me to refine my discipline. I poured into my work, my teams, and my development. For over a decade, I ranked at the top. But the true accomplishment was not the recognition. It was the growth. I was becoming a man who lived intentionally because the cost of not doing so had become too great.

While my career was rising, my internal world still needed refinement. I faced personal failures that exposed the parts of me that discipline alone could not fix. I had to develop emotional discipline. Relational discipline. Spiritual discipline. I had to learn how to lead myself not only through pressure, but through healing.

That journey eventually led me into the world of coaching. After years of traditional therapy, it was one coaching session that broke through everything I had spent years holding together. The questions forced me into a level of introspection no one had ever guided me through. It was raw. It was painful. It was freeing. Afterwards, all I knew was that I wanted to help others navigate their internal landscape the same way someone helped me.

Coaching taught me that purpose expands when discipline matures. You cannot live a purposeful life if your habits contradict your healing. You cannot lead others if you have not built structure around your own growth. You cannot live fully if you keep returning to cycles that diminish your identity.

This chapter is not about discipline for discipline's sake. It is about building the life God intended for you, one intentional step at a time. It is about creating habits that reflect your values. It is about practicing the kind of consistency that strengthens your identity. It is about developing the discipline to become the version of yourself your purpose requires.

Your discipline is not about perfection.

It is about formation.

It is about shaping your identity with intention.

It is about aligning your habits with your calling.

It is about becoming someone capable of carrying the purpose placed within you.

Every day you practice discipline, you are adding another piece to the person you are becoming. You are absorbing every lesson, every mistake, every breakthrough, every moment of clarity, every act of courage, every whisper of purpose. You are building your life with intention, not accident.

That is how discipline and purpose begin to agree with each other.

And that is the essence of becoming the sum.

Chapter 11 SUM IT UP

THE SUM FRAMEWORK: SEE + UNDERSTAND + MANIFEST

Every time you abandoned yourself, you drifted further from purpose. This is where you return to you.

SEE: where you chose others over yourself.

UNDERSTAND: what that decision cost you.

MANIFEST: integrity by honoring your needs.

BECOMING THE SUM:

1. Where did you betray your own needs?

2. Why did you do it?

3. How can you honor yourself today?

THE SUM CHALLENGE:

Choose yourself in one decision today.

PRAYER FOR THE JOURNEY:

God, help me walk in integrity and honor who You created me to be. Amen.

"Presence speaks long before your words ever will."

CHAPTER 12

OWNING YOUR BECOMING

There is a moment in every person's transformation when growth stops being a possibility and starts becoming an identity. It does not happen in a dramatic flash of clarity or in a single triumphant victory. It happens quietly, in the everyday choices you make to rise a little higher than the version of yourself you have known. Owning your becoming is the moment you stop apologizing for your evolution and start embracing it.

For many people, this moment is the hardest part of the journey. It is one thing to desire change. It is another to accept what that change reveals. Growth requires you to release the old patterns that once protected you. It requires you to set boundaries with people who prefer the version of you that needed them. It requires you to acknowledge the dreams you buried because you feared they were too big or too painful to revisit. Owning your becoming is not simply stepping into a new life. It is letting go of the life you have outgrown.

When I look back at the seasons where I was rebuilding, I can see how often I resisted my own growth. I wanted healing, but I feared what it might demand from me. I wanted purpose, but I was hesitant to accept the responsibility that came with it. I wanted transformation, but I was still learning how to feel worthy of it. Many people live in this same tension. They want to become more…

but something inside them clings to the safety of who they used to be.

Owning your becoming means confronting the insecurity that whispers you are not enough. It means recognizing the voice of doubt that tries to convince you that your past disqualifies you from your future. It means resisting the urge to shrink yourself so others feel comfortable. It means acknowledging that your growth may outpace the environments and relationships that once felt familiar. Your becoming will challenge the fears that shaped you. It will challenge the limitations you accepted. It will challenge the stories you told yourself to make sense of past pain.

The first step in owning your becoming is acknowledging that growth will change the way people perceive you. Some will celebrate it. Some will feel threatened by it. Some will distance themselves from it. Others will try to pull you back into who you used to be. This does not mean they are wrong or malicious. It simply means your transformation highlights where others are still avoiding their own. People who knew the older version of you may not understand the newer version you are building. And that is okay.

The second step is learning to embrace your new identity with confidence. When your discipline strengthens, your habits evolve, your clarity increases, and your purpose expands, you will begin to recognize the difference between who you were and who you are becoming. That recognition can feel unfamiliar. You may question if you deserve success, peace, or purpose. You may question if your voice matters. You may question if you are ready. But growth does not wait for you to feel fully qualified. Growth responds to your willingness.

The third step is accepting that your becoming will require courage. It takes courage to let go of the labels you once accepted. It takes courage to change the environments that shaped your identity. It takes courage to admit that you want more out of life. It takes courage to claim a future that feels bigger than your past. Courage is the decision to move with honesty despite the fear.

As I grew in my career, my purpose, and my spiritual maturity, I began to release the version of myself that was built solely around performance. I stopped defining myself by what I accomplished and instead focused on who I was becoming. I learned to embrace the parts of me that had been shaped by pain, resilience, and faith. My identity became less about survival and more about intention. And as I embraced that identity, the people I served grew with me.

Your becoming will not always feel linear. Some days you will feel grounded and strong. Other days you will feel like you are slipping back into old habits or old thoughts. This does not mean you are failing. It means you are human. Growth is not a straight line. It is a series of choices, reflections, and recommitments. The important part is that you keep returning to the version of yourself you are building.

This chapter invites you to honor your own evolution. You have survived things that once tried to break you. You have learned lessons that reshaped your character. You have outgrown beliefs that once kept you small. You have stepped into a level of awareness that many people never reach. Your becoming is not accidental. It is intentional. It is purposeful. It is sacred.

Owning your becoming means stepping fully into the identity that God has been shaping within you since the beginning. It means recognizing that everything you have lived through, everything you have healed from, everything you have learned, and everything you have risen above has prepared you for this moment. The more you embrace your becoming, the more you align with the purpose placed inside you.

Every step you take toward your new identity adds to the story of who you are becoming. Every act of courage, every moment of clarity, every boundary you set, and every truth you confront becomes part of the greater sum of your life.

You are learning to trust the person God is forming in you now, not only the person you had to be to survive.

And that is the essence of becoming the sum.

Chapter 12 SUM IT UP

THE SUM FRAMEWORK: SEE + UNDERSTAND + MANIFEST

Your triggers are signals. They point to the parts of you that still need attention.

SEE: the reactions that rise quickly in you.

UNDERSTAND: the story behind those reactions.

MANIFEST: clarity by choosing a healthy response.

BECOMING THE SUM:

1. What reaction do you have that surprises you?

2. What is the real story behind it?

3. What healthier response can you practice?

THE SUM CHALLENGE:

Notice one trigger today and slow down before responding.

PRAYER FOR THE JOURNEY:

God, help me understand my reactions and respond with wisdom and peace. Amen.

"Purpose is the assignment your life has been preparing you for."

CHAPTER 13

LEADING FROM WITHIN

There is a moment in every leader's life when influence stops being something you chase and becomes something you carry. It arrives quietly, not with recognition or applause, but with the realization that the strength you built in private has begun to steady the people around you. This is not the kind of leadership that announces itself. It is the leadership that forms when your inner world becomes strong enough to guide others through their fear, their uncertainty, and their suffering.

For many people, leadership feels like something external. A title. A rank. A position. But true influence begins long before any of that. It begins in the places where your character is shaped without witnesses. It begins in the moments when you choose responsibility over comfort. It begins in the seasons when you learn to carry more than just your own weight.

One of the clearest moments of leadership in my life did not happen in a classroom or an office or during a promotion ceremony. It happened in the middle of a multi day combat operation that pushed every one of us past our physical and emotional limits. We moved through terrain where every step was a question. The dirt beneath my boots crunched in a way that made me wonder if something was buried below the surface waiting to detonate. My shoulders ached under the weight of my gear. The straps dug into my muscles. The helmet pressed into my skull and sent sharp headaches through the back of my head. The night vision devices strained my eyes until my temples pulsed.

We had gone black on water more than once. Everything was rationed. Sweat dried into salt on our uniforms and then returned as new sweat the moment we moved again. When one person had even a few ounces left in their camelback, we shared across the squad because thirst was not something anyone could afford alone. Exhaustion hit us in ways I cannot fully describe. It was not simply fatigue. It was the slow erosion of the body and mind while still being expected to operate with precision.

We were being shot at from directions we could not always identify. The air cracked with bullets as they snapped past our ears. The smell of gunpowder mixed with dust settled in our throats. Every movement required courage. Every pause required awareness. Every decision required discipline. In one compound we cleared, there was a full watermelon patch growing in the dirt courtyard. I picked up one of the watermelons before someone yelled for me to STOP. The entire patch had been daisy chained with multiple improvised explosive devices. The simplicity of the trap made it more horrifying than anything else. It was a reminder that one moment of comfort could cost you your life.

But what struck me most during those days outside of the danger, was what I saw in the faces of the men around me. We were all suffering. Each man carried his own fear, his own pain, his own exhaustion. Some limped. Some moved slower. Some fought through injuries none of us had time to treat. And the more I watched them, the more something inside me shifted. My own discomfort, my own fear, my own exhaustion began to matter less. I wanted nothing more than to see them suffer less. I wanted to make their load lighter. I wanted to shield them from the weight that was crushing all of us.

That was the moment I understood something that changed my entire view of leadership. Leadership is not about the leader. Leadership is about responsibility for the people entrusted to you. It is about becoming strong enough internally so that others can borrow your strength externally. It is about remaining steady when circumstances are chaotic. It is about suffering well so others can suffer less. That operation revealed the kind of leader I wanted to be. Not a leader who commanded attention, but a leader who carried others.

In that environment, I realized that my inner life was no longer private. It was equipment my brothers needed me to bring to the fight.

This same principle applies outside of combat. In classrooms. In corporations. In families. On teams. In relationships. Every person has moments where someone around them is struggling silently. Someone is afraid. Someone is uncertain. Someone is carrying a weight they do not know how to name. Leading from within means being the person who sees it. The person who steadies the room. The person who listens without judgment. The person who takes one step closer instead of stepping away.

Leadership becomes dangerous when people think it begins with authority. Leadership begins with awareness. It begins with character. It begins with empathy. It begins when your identity aligns with your responsibility. When you become someone others trust, not because of what you say, but because of who you are when no one is watching.

As I continued to grow in my life and career, I realized that the most influential leaders are not the ones who seek followers. They are the ones who elevate the people around them. They are the ones who stay calm when others panic. They are the ones who make others feel capable when doubt begins to rise. They are the ones whose presence reduces fear. Not because they are fearless, but because they have learned how to lead themselves through fear.

Leading from within also means accepting that your transformation will impact people long before you notice it. Your discipline becomes a guide for others. Your healing becomes a permission slip for others to heal. Your steadiness becomes an anchor for those who feel unsteady. Your compassion becomes a pathway for those who have forgotten how to soften without breaking.

Eventually, influence becomes less about what you accomplish and more about who you become. A leader's identity shapes their environment. A leader's character shapes their culture. A leader's presence shapes their people. Leadership is not something you put on. It is something you grow into from the inside out.

Take a moment and reflect on the spaces you walk into every day.

Do people feel calmer when you arrive or more tense?

Do they feel supported or overlooked?

Do they feel encouraged or depleted?

Do they feel seen or ignored?

Who are you becoming when others need someone steady to stand beside them?

Your ability to lead others will always be a reflection of your willingness to lead yourself. The more you strengthen your inner world, the more your outer influence begins to expand. Every lesson you have lived, every moment of suffering, every breakthrough, every burden, every victory, and every scar becomes part of the leader you are becoming.

This is what it means to lead from within.

This is what it means to honor the people you serve.

And this is what it means to become the sum.

Chapter 13 SUM IT UP

THE SUM FRAMEWORK: SEE + UNDERSTAND + MANIFEST

Walls feel safe until they keep you from real connection.

SEE: where you closed your heart.

UNDERSTAND: what made you protect yourself.

MANIFEST: connection by showing a little more of who you are.

BECOMING THE SUM:

1. Where have you been guarded?

2. What caused you to shut down?

3. What small step toward connection can you take?

THE SUM CHALLENGE:

Let someone you trust in just a little more today.

PRAYER FOR THE JOURNEY:

God, help me open my heart in the places where I once shut down. Amen.

"You rise to the level of the standards you enforce, not the ones you speak."

CHAPTER 14

THE RISING STANDARD

Every leader reaches a moment when their growth must rise to match the weight of what they have been entrusted with. It does not happen suddenly. It builds quietly, often in the background, through experiences that shape your perception of who you are and who you are becoming. One day you realize the decisions you make influence more than your own life. The standard you keep becomes the foundation others stand on. Your presence becomes something people rely on more than you may ever hear them admit. This is the moment when growth stops being optional and becomes stewardship.

You may feel it as a subtle pull toward greater discipline. You may feel it as the quiet awareness that people look to you, even if they never say it out loud. You may feel it when you walk into rooms and notice that others adjust their confidence, their energy, or their expectations based on how you show up. Leadership grows in these moments long before anyone calls you a leader.

My own shift began in a season when my responsibilities were changing in ways I did not anticipate. I had spent years becoming competent, driven, and resilient. But competence alone cannot carry purpose. At a certain point in my life, excellence stopped being about what I could achieve and began to reflect the lives connected to my decisions. It became clear that leadership was not something I simply expressed. It was something I was becoming responsible for.

That truth became undeniable the day I sat across from a senior officer during one of my early coaching sessions in Special Operations. He entered the room with the posture of someone used to carrying authority. His career was full of accomplishments. His reputation stretched across organizations. Yet when the door closed, the weight behind his eyes told a different story.

He began by discussing leadership challenges, but the tone of his voice revealed something deeper. People often speak around their pain before they ever speak from it. When I asked a question that touched the center of his struggle, he paused. The entire room shifted in that silence. He no longer spoke as a leader defending a position. He spoke as a man confronting a truth he had avoided for years.

He talked about the pressure of being the person everyone depended on, while having no space in his life where he could express vulnerability. He talked about expectations that never seemed to lessen, no matter how much he accomplished. He talked about feeling trapped between who he was required to be and who he actually was beneath the responsibilities.

As he spoke, the weight he carried began to surface. His voice faltered. His eyes filled. And for the first time in a very long time, he allowed himself to be honest. Not for the sake of performance, but for the sake of healing.

I did not give him advice. Leadership at that level does not need more instruction. It needs clarity. It needs space. It needs truth spoken without fear of judgment. I helped him explore what he had been avoiding, not by telling him what to do, but by helping him hear the voice he had been ignoring inside himself. Sometimes the greatest service a leader can offer is presence strong enough for someone else to finally exhale.

When the session ended, he shook my hand with a sincerity that said more than his words. He thanked me, not for solutions, but for the safety to finally admit what he could not say anywhere else. When he walked out of the room, I sat in the quiet that followed, realizing that leadership had expanded again. Not outwardly, but inwardly. Not through achievement, but through presence. Not through authority, but through the trust of another human being.

That day changed me. It revealed that leadership does not reach its highest form through performance or pressure. It reaches its highest form when your life becomes a place where others can grow. When your steadiness becomes a turning point for someone who has carried too much alone. When your integrity creates space for someone to speak truth without fear. When your maturity strengthens someone who is quietly unraveling. This is leadership measured not by output, but by impact.

Leadership becomes purpose when what you carry helps others stand tall.

From that day forward, I understood that my calling required more than capability. It required depth. It required empathy. It required character. It required spiritual alignment. It required becoming someone who could hold space for transformation without needing recognition. It required a standard that matched the magnitude of what God was entrusting me with.

This is where the SUM Model comes into focus again. You must SEE the weight of your influence, UNDERSTAND the lives it touches, and MANIFEST a standard that honors that responsibility.

This chapter is where your own rising standard begins. In the truth that the world around you changes when you choose to grow with intention. Someone is watching how you navigate disappointment. Someone is learning from how you respond under pressure. Someone is encouraged by how you pursue healing. Someone is finding courage in the example you set without even realizing it.

Leadership is measured by the strength of the lives influenced by your presence. And as your awareness grows, your responsibility grows with it.

Who is looking to you for reassurance?

Who draws strength from your consistency?

Who gains direction because you remain steady?

Who finds clarity because you choose to grow?

Who becomes braver because you refuse to shrink?

Your calling is shaped by more than your gifts.

It is shaped by the discipline to rise into the person others can trust.

It is shaped by the humility to continue becoming.

It is shaped by the courage to face your truth with honesty.

It is shaped by the grace God places over your life when you step into purpose with obedience.

Leadership deepens when you recognize that your life carries weight beyond your own.

This is where stewardship begins.

This is where calling matures.

This is where your influence becomes legacy.

This is where you stop leading for today and begin leading for the generations connected to your life.

This is where you become the sum.

Chapter 14 SUM IT UP

THE SUM FRAMEWORK: SEE + UNDERSTAND + MANIFEST

God's instruction often arrives before your confidence does. Trust the direction.

SEE: what God has been nudging you to do.

UNDERSTAND: why you've hesitated.

MANIFEST: obedience through action.

BECOMING THE SUM:

1. What has God placed on your heart?

2. What fear is slowing you down?

3. What step of obedience can you take right now?

THE SUM CHALLENGE:

Take the step that God already confirmed.

PRAYER FOR THE JOURNEY:

God, give me courage to follow Your direction without hesitation. Amen.

"Purpose hunts you long before you learn how to recognize its voice."

CHAPTER 15

WHEN PURPOSE FINDS YOU FIRST

Purpose does not always arrive with clarity or confidence. Sometimes it arrives disguised as a burden. Sometimes it appears through the pain of others. Sometimes it breaks your heart before it opens your eyes. And sometimes it finds you long before you feel ready to carry it.

There are stages of growth every person passes through.

The first stage is survival. You learn how to carry yourself. You learn how to make it through the day. You learn how to quiet your own storms.

The second stage is development. You begin strengthening the parts of yourself that were once fragile. You sharpen your discipline. You improve your habits. You grow in capability and confidence.

The third stage is where leadership is born. It is the moment when life places you in front of people whose battles pull something deeper out of you. It is where responsibility takes shape. It is where you realize you are no longer growing only for yourself.

I reached that stage the moment I understood that my purpose was tied to the pain of others.

I watched my own family fight battles they did not choose. I saw the emotional exhaustion in their eyes. I saw the weight of generational wounds that did not belong to them yet still clung to them. I realized that leadership inside a home is just as courageous as leadership on any battlefield. It takes spiritual strength to hold a family together. It takes emotional maturity to notice when someone you love is sinking quietly.

Their struggles awakened something in me that survival had never accessed. It taught me that purpose will always demand a deeper version of you than comfort ever will. It made me understand that leadership begins with the people closest to you.

Then came the juvenile detention centers. I walked into those rooms expecting hardened youth. Instead I saw children. Worn down. Disconnected. Searching for belonging in places that only deepened their hurt. I met an eight-year-old boy whose body was marked with tattoos. He was small. Soft-spoken. His eyes carried a lifetime of experiences no child should ever carry. He told me he did not want to leave the system because the system felt safer than the world outside. Hearing that at his age did something to my spirit. It forced me to confront a truth many leaders avoid. People are not always fighting for success. Some are fighting simply to survive their circumstances. Purpose will always show you suffering before it shows you strategy.

I did not walk out of that building thinking about leadership principles. I walked out with a spiritual weight that sat in my chest for days. I started asking myself what kind of leader I needed to become to speak life into people who had been convinced their future was already decided.

Then I met students in classrooms who were brilliant but lost. They turned in assignments yet felt no purpose. They acted out not because they wanted attention but because they were calling out for direction. Their misbehavior was communication. Their silence was communication. Their hunger for identity was communication. And I saw myself in some of them. I saw the lost boy who once believed anger was strength because he did not yet understand hurt. Their cries for meaning became another reminder that leadership is not about rules. It is about recognition. People do not follow you because you demand it. They follow because you see them.

Purpose pushed deeper when I thought about my teammates in Special Operations. I spent countless nights working long after everyone else went to sleep. Not because anyone required it. Not because it would earn me praise. But because I knew what it felt like to be in chaos. I knew what it felt like to march into danger with uncertainty as your silent companion. If my preparation could provide even a moment of clarity for someone else, it mattered. I wanted them to rest easier. I wanted them to trust their environment. I wanted them to feel supported even when life did not allow them to say it out loud.

Leadership in those spaces was not a position. It was a choice to serve even when no one was watching. Purpose grows fastest in the dark, long before anyone sees the work you are doing.

But the weight became heaviest when I began losing people. Not strangers. Not acquaintances. Friends. Brothers. A family member. People who still had chapters left to live. People who still had purpose inside them. People whose stories were not supposed to end when they did. Five friends lost to suicide. Five lives that should still be here. Their deaths did not create emptiness. They created responsibility. They made me confront a truth I could no longer ignore.

There are people in the world who will not survive if leaders do not show up whole, present, spiritually grounded, and equipped.

Their absence became part of my calling.

This is why my relationship with God deepened. I realized I was being shaped for work that required more than discipline. It required discernment. It required compassion. It required humility. It required obedience. It required a willingness to grow in ways that were uncomfortable but necessary. Leadership stopped being a career pursuit and became a spiritual assignment. When I looked back, I could trace back how every battle had prepared me for that assignment. The more I paid attention, the more I recognized the pattern. Every painful moment in my life had prepared me to stand in gaps that others could not.

Excellence became my offering.

Growth became my stewardship.

Discipline became my service.

Healing became my preparation.

I did not master my craft for applause. I mastered it because someone needed the strongest version of me.

I studied relentlessly because I knew purpose cannot be fulfilled on half-developed potential.

I pushed myself because I was tired of burying friends who believed they had nothing left to give. I refused to allow anyone connected to my assignment to slip silently into despair.

Leadership shifted from ambition to responsibility.

From performance to purpose.

From self-focus to spiritual clarity.

From doing to becoming.

Purpose finds you the moment you recognize that your strength is not for you. Your influence is not for you. Your journey is not for you. Your life is tied to lives you have not even met yet. And leadership becomes transformational when you understand that your calling is bigger than your comfort. You are becoming someone whose presence carries impact. You are becoming someone who can shift an environment simply by showing up whole. You are becoming someone God can trust with the weight of other people's breakthroughs.

This is what it means to step into purpose.

This is what it means to grow into calling.

This is what it means to become the sum.

When purpose finds you first, it never lets you go.

Chapter 15 SUM IT UP

THE SUM FRAMEWORK: SEE + UNDERSTAND + MANIFEST

Your gifts were given to you for a reason. Use them well.

SEE: the strength God placed in you.

UNDERSTAND: the purpose behind it.

MANIFEST: excellence by using your gift intentionally.

BECOMING THE SUM:

1. What gift do you overlook?

2. Why have you held it back?

3. How can you use it today?

THE SUM CHALLENGE:

Apply your gift once with full intention.

PRAYER FOR THE JOURNEY:

God, show me how to use my gifts with clarity and excellence. Amen.

PART II

THE RISE OF PURPOSE-DRIVEN LEADERSHIP

"Legacy begins the moment your leadership becomes bigger than you."

CHAPTER 16

THE SHIFT INTO LEGACY LEADERSHIP

Legacy does not begin the day you grow old. It begins the day you recognize that your life is shaping more than your own story. Every decision you make sends a ripple into the future. Every word you speak becomes a seed. Every habit you choose becomes a pattern someone else will follow. People think legacy is about being remembered, but it is not about memory. It is about impact. It is about influence that survives you. It is about becoming the kind of person whose presence reaches into places your feet may never stand. Legacy is the quiet proof that your becoming is not only for you.

There is a moment when leadership stops being about progress and starts being about inheritance. Not inheritance measured in money, but inheritance measured in character, identity, discipline, faith, and purpose. Legacy leadership is something you build with intention. It is the point in your journey where you understand that your growth has a future attached to it. Everything you cultivate internally becomes something someone else depends on externally.

I began understanding legacy the day I realized the world does not wait for you to be perfect before it starts learning from you. My children were watching long before I was ready to be watched. Their eyes studied the way I handled pressure. Their ears listened to the tone I used when life demanded something from me. Their hearts absorbed the atmosphere I created, even in moments they were too young to understand.

It is humbling when you realize that your weaknesses can become someone else's struggle. Your anger can become someone else's pattern. Your silence can become someone else's fear. Your avoidance can become someone else's insecurity. But the opposite is also true. Your strength can become someone else's foundation. Your discipline can become someone else's identity. Your faith can become someone else's anchor. Your purpose can become someone else's roadmap. Your transformation becomes a living example of what is possible. Legacy leadership starts with taking ownership of what your life is already teaching.

Legacy leadership begins with awareness.

I felt the weight of this deeply when I began working with young people. There were students who reminded me of versions of myself I had forgotten. They were brilliant but unfocused. Hurt but hiding. Present but disconnected. They carried dreams with no direction, potential with no mentorship, and frustration with no language to express what they were experiencing. Some were angry because anger was the only emotion they believed was allowed. Others were quiet because silence was safer than being misunderstood.

I remember standing in front of them one day and thinking to myself, they do not need perfection from me. They need presence. They need conviction. They need consistency. They need someone willing to invest in them even when the world calls them difficult. They need someone who can see beyond their behavior and into their identity. That moment awakened a new sense of responsibility inside me. I realized that leadership is not about managing people. It is about leaving people better than you found them. Legacy begins in the unseen ways you lift others without expecting anything in return.

The same truth showed up in my work with families, Soldiers, and teams across every environment I entered. People were not looking for someone flawless. They were looking for someone faithful. Someone who lived the values they taught. Someone who held themselves to a standard that inspired others to rise. Someone who showed what excellence looked like when no one was clapping. Someone whose life whispered, you can become more.

Legacy leadership is not loud. It is formed in the small moments that shape culture. It shows up in the way you treat people who cannot offer you anything. It shows up in the way you recover after you fail. It shows up in the way you respond to pressure, temptation, disappointment, and opportunity. Legacy is built in the consistency that the world rarely sees but deeply feels.

I understood this even more deeply when I encountered people whose lives were collapsing under battles they did not choose. Some were young. Some were older. Some had every gift imaginable yet felt purposeless. Others were fighting addiction, loneliness, fear, or hopelessness. The more people I encountered, the more I realized that leadership is generational stewardship.

You are responsible for raising the standard in ways that lift others out of places you once struggled to escape.

Your healing becomes a bridge. Your strength becomes refuge. Your courage becomes instruction.

Legacy leadership demands spiritual growth. Without God guiding your identity, your influence becomes unstable. Without healing, your habits become harmful. Without purpose, your leadership becomes shallow. Without direction, your impact becomes accidental instead of intentional. Legacy leadership requires depth, not noise. It requires conviction, not applause. It requires alignment, not ambition.

As I watched my children grow, as I coached leaders, and as I walked alongside people fighting for hope, I realized that the future is shaped one decision at a time. Legacy is not built in grand gestures. It is built in daily choices. The decision to be honest. The decision to be present. The decision to forgive. The decision to speak life. The decision to grow even when no one notices. The decision to show up as the person you needed when you were younger.

If you want to know what kind of legacy you are building, look at what your life teaches in silence.

Who are you when no one is watching?

What is the standard you set for yourself?

What is the atmosphere you create around others?

What part of your story are people learning from without you realizing it?

What do your actions say about your priorities?

What will continue to grow because you planted it?

These questions are meant to create perspective, not pressure. You are shaping the future every single day. You are influencing people you may never meet. You are contributing to a story bigger than your own. This is what it means to carry legacy.

As you turn this page, take a moment to reflect on the truth that sits at the center of generational leadership. Your life is becoming the blueprint for someone else's breakthrough. Your discipline is becoming someone else's direction. Your healing is becoming someone else's courage. And your faith is becoming someone else's hope.

This is the shift into legacy leadership.

You begin to SEE your impact, UNDERSTAND its reach, and MANIFEST a standard that outlives you.

This is what it means to become the sum.

Chapter 16 SUM IT UP

THE SUM FRAMEWORK: SEE + UNDERSTAND + MANIFEST

Growth requires honesty. You cannot carry old identities into new assignments.

SEE: the version of you that no longer fits.

UNDERSTAND: why you held onto it.

MANIFEST: confidence by stepping into the new.

BECOMING THE SUM:

1. What old identity are you done carrying?

2. Why did it feel safe?

3. What action reflects who you are becoming?

THE SUM CHALLENGE:

Act today as your future self, not your former self.

PRAYER FOR THE JOURNEY:

God, reveal who I am becoming and guide me into that identity with confidence. Amen.

"Vision requires the courage to build in the dark before others
see the light."

CHAPTER 17

.

THE COURAGE TO BUILD WHAT OTHERS CANNOT SEE

Influence is not merely the ability to move people. It is the ability to shape environments so deeply that others rise because you walked into a room. It is the power to elevate the standard without announcing that the standard has changed. It is service in action. It is vision in motion. It is the willingness to build something that does not yet exist so others can experience a future they did not believe was possible.

Every meaningful transformation in history began with someone who saw what others could not. Someone who refused to accept "normal" as the limit. Someone who understood that leadership is not about echoing what already exists. It is about creating what is missing. It is about shaping culture instead of adjusting to it. It is about having the courage to break patterns, to speak life, to introduce new possibilities, and to stand for values long before they are appreciated.

That is what influence truly is. Not authority. Not position. Influence is the quiet force of a transformed life that begins transforming others.

Many of the places I worked throughout my career were environments where excellence was expected but humanity was often forgotten. Pressure was high. Stakes were real. People were tired. Some were quietly breaking. Others were drowning behind strong faces. It would have been easy to focus only on performance and ignore the people carrying the weight. But leadership rooted in service sees what others overlook.

My influence grew the moment I started trying to improve. I realized that every environment I entered had a temperature, and it was my responsibility to set it, not adapt to it. Instead of letting pressure dictate my posture, I began shaping the atmosphere around me. I created certainty where there was confusion. I created stability where there was anxiety. I created direction where there was hesitation. And I did it consistently enough that people began to rely on it.

Influence is not loud. It is consistent.

I saw this clearly the night I stayed awake working while others rested. I was exhausted. Everyone was. But there was something inside me that refused to let the team step into a mission with uncertainty hanging over them. I could not remove the danger. I could not promise safety. But I could give them clarity. I could prepare them with precision. I could take the weight off their minds even if I had to carry it myself.

That is service.

And service is the birthplace of influence.

But leadership does not end with making environments better. It continues with building futures that do not yet exist.

The most transformational leaders are builders. They build culture. They build confidence. They build systems. They build people. They build possibilities. They build futures others have never imagined. They stand in the gap between what is and what should be, and they refuse to step back.

Some of the most important things I ever built were not programs or plans. They were people. People who had given up on themselves. People who believed their story was over. People who thought they had peaked. People who felt invisible. People who needed a voice stronger than their doubt.

I coached Soldiers who had forgotten their strength. I mentored students who had never been told their life had purpose. I worked with children in schools and detention centers who had been hurt so deeply that they believed survival was the highest goal they could achieve. I guided leaders who were carrying pain in private while trying to appear invincible in public.

I realized that building people was sacred work. It required empathy. It required vision. It required courage. Most of all, it required the ability to see beyond what was in front of you.

If influence is the ability to elevate a moment, building is the ability to elevate a future.

You cannot become a builder without courage. Building something new means stepping away from what is familiar. It means being misunderstood. It means being challenged. It means standing for values no one applauds yet. It means investing in people who may not see their own worth until much later. It means creating structures, habits, and culture that others may take for granted but cannot live without.

True builders are not motivated by reward. They are motivated by responsibility.

Leadership becomes powerful when you understand that someone else's freedom, growth, identity, or destiny may depend on the foundation you lay today. The work you put in now may become the structure they stand on later. Your courage may become the reason someone else finds theirs.

As you read this, consider the world you are shaping by the way you show up. You may not realize it, but your presence is creating patterns. Your decisions are constructing buildings. Your habits are forming foundations. Your compassion is carving pathways. Your strength is opening doors. Your discipline is lighting the way for people who would have remained in darkness without you.

This is the calling of transformational leadership.

It is not only lived. It is built.

It is not only seen. It is shaped.

It is not only felt. It is carried forward.

You are not simply influencing today.

You are constructing tomorrow.

And everything you build becomes part of someone else's becoming.

This is the heart of visionary leadership.

This is the courage to create what has never existed.

This is the commitment to serve at a level that changes lives.

This is where you learn to SEE what is missing, UNDERSTAND what it could become, and MANIFEST it with courage.

This is how you begin becoming the sum.

Chapter 17 SUM IT UP

THE SUM FRAMEWORK: SEE + UNDERSTAND + MANIFEST

Resistance shows up right before growth breaks through.

SEE: what you keep putting off.

UNDERSTAND: the fear or doubt behind it.

MANIFEST: discipline by taking a step forward.

BECOMING THE SUM:

1. What are you delaying?

2. What is the real reason behind it?

3. What step can you take today?

THE SUM CHALLENGE:

Move toward the thing you've been resisting.

PRAYER FOR THE JOURNEY:

God, steady me when I resist growth and help me move with courage. Amen.

"You teach people how to lead by the atmosphere you bring into the room."

CHAPTER 18

THE ENVIRONMENT YOU CREATE

Every leader carries an atmosphere with them. You bring it into rooms, homes, teams, classrooms, workplaces, and relationships. Long before you speak, people feel the environment you create. They feel your steadiness or your tension, your clarity or your confusion, your peace or your chaos. Leadership is not only what you do. It is the atmosphere you cultivate in the spaces you move through.

Some people create pressure wherever they go. Others create ease. Some create fear. Others create courage. Some create silence. Others create belonging. The environment you create becomes the silent teacher in every room you enter. People may forget your words, but they remember how the space felt when you arrived.

True leadership begins when you take responsibility for the environment you shape.

I learned this long before I understood it. There were seasons in my life where chaos followed me everywhere, and I did not yet have the emotional awareness to understand why. I was hurting, moving too fast, reacting instead of responding, carrying unresolved wounds into every space I stepped into. The environments around me reflected it. People walked lighter when I left the room. They braced themselves when I entered. My inner world was shaping the outer world, and I had not learned how to steward it.

Growth changed that.

As I healed, my atmosphere shifted. I began learning how to carry calm into stressful moments. I began learning how to create trust in places filled with uncertainty. I began learning how to communicate without elevating tension. I began learning how to bring direction to rooms filled with confusion. The more responsibility I carried, the more I realized that leadership is less about commanding people and more about shaping environments that bring out the best in them. Healing altered my presence, and my presence altered the climate of every room I entered.

I saw this clearly when working with teams in high-stakes environments. There were nights when pressure weighed on us so heavily that breathing felt like effort. People were tired, stretched thin, second-guessing themselves, and trying to find stability in shifting conditions. I realized that if I arrived anxious, the entire room absorbed it. If I arrived steady, the room softened. If I arrived focused, the team aligned. My presence set the temperature.

People perform differently when someone carries peace into a storm.

I saw the same pattern as an instructor and teacher in Special Operations. Those who were distracted were not responding to content. They were responding to the environment. They needed safety before they needed instruction. They needed connection before they needed correction. The tone of the room mattered more than the curriculum. When I walked in with warmth and presence, their posture changed. When I walked in with heaviness, they withdrew. Atmosphere shaped behavior, not the other way around.

I saw it with my own children as well. They mirrored my energy, even when I wished they would not. If my tone was sharp, they became guarded. If my pace was rushed, they grew anxious. If my presence was steady, they felt safe. Leadership within a family is one of the clearest mirrors you will ever face. It reveals the environment you create more honestly than any professional setting ever will.

And I saw it with leaders across all walks of life. Some operated from insecurity, and their teams carried that insecurity like a hidden weight. Some operated from fear, and their teams second-guessed every move. Some operated from ego, and their teams walked on eggshells. But leaders who operated from internal stability created environments where people flourished. They built places where others could think, grow, speak, and lead without fear of failure or judgment.

The environment you create becomes your legacy long before your words do.

Every leader must learn to carry certain things with them intentionally. Patience. Presence. Humility. Conviction. Clarity. Honor. Emotional steadiness. Spiritual awareness. These qualities shape environments more than directives ever will. When you carry these things consistently, people begin to trust you without being asked. They begin to contribute at a higher level. They begin to grow alongside you instead of behind you.

Creating the right environment does not mean eliminating conflict or discomfort. It means creating space where growth is possible. It means cultivating a culture where people feel safe to bring their ideas, their questions, and even their mistakes. It means speaking with consistency. Listening with compassion. Leading with conviction. Holding a standard that does not waver depending on mood or stress. It means living with emotional and spiritual discipline so others do not have to absorb the weight of battles you have not resolved.

Your atmosphere becomes your leadership.

This chapter exists to remind you of something crucial. The environment you create is not a reflection of circumstance. It is a reflection of character. And character can be developed.

Healed.

Strengthened.

Sharpened.

Transformed.

You are not bound to the atmosphere you once created. You are capable of shaping something far more powerful, far more uplifting, and far more aligned with the leader you are becoming.

As you turn the page, remember that leadership is not only about what you accomplish. It is about what you cultivate. It is about the emotional and spiritual temperature you set everywhere you go. It is about shaping environments where others can rise into the fullness of who they were meant to be.

This is the art of atmosphere.

This is the calling of transformational leadership.

This is how you continue becoming the sum.

Chapter 18 SUM IT UP

THE SUM FRAMEWORK: SEE + UNDERSTAND + MANIFEST

Sometimes you forget how far you've come. Pause and honor the progress.

SEE: your growth.

UNDERSTAND: the sacrifice behind it.

MANIFEST: gratitude in how you show up.

BECOMING THE SUM:

1. What progress are you overlooking?

2. What did it require of you?

3. How can you honor your growth today?

THE SUM CHALLENGE:

Acknowledge your progress with intention.

PRAYER FOR THE JOURNEY:

God, help me see my growth clearly and honor the work that shaped me. Amen.

"Transition is alignment with who you are becoming."

CHAPTER 19

ALIGNMENT IN THE SEASONS OF TRANSITION

There are moments in life when standing still feels impossible. Moments when the identity you have carried for years begins to loosen its grip. Moments when the path that once felt clear begins to shift beneath your feet. These moments are not signs of failure. They are signs of transition. They are invitations for alignment. They are reminders that purpose evolves, and so must you.

Leadership is not only defined by what you step into. It is also defined by what you are willing to release.

Most people resist transition because they misunderstand it. They see it as loss instead of refinement. They see it as instability instead of expansion. They see it as endings instead of preparation. Yet some of the most crucial seasons of leadership are shaped during transitions that feel uncomfortable, unfamiliar, and unplanned.

Transition is the moment when God separates who you were from who you are becoming.

This process requires spiritual alignment more than anything else. If your identity is rooted in a title, a uniform, a role, or a season, transition will break you. But if your identity is rooted in God, transition becomes an unveiling. It becomes the moment where layers fall away. Where outdated patterns detach. Where your spirit becomes clear, still, and ready for the next assignment.

There was a time when my entire identity was tied to the uniform I wore. I spent years becoming excellent in my craft. Years building influence. Years serving at the highest levels. My name carried weight. My performance opened doors. My discipline shaped culture. But the deeper I went into purpose, the more God began pulling me toward something beyond the identity I had built.

It felt unsettling at first. Even confusing. But God often calls you out of what is familiar before He reveals what is next.

That is the tension of transition. You feel the pull before you can explain it. You feel the shift before you can name it. You feel the stir in your spirit before you understand its direction. And if you are not aligned with God, you will cling to a season He is trying to move you out of.

Transition requires trust.

Alignment requires surrender.

Years ago when I began approaching the idea or need of retirement from the military, I felt the weight of everything changing. For years, the mission was clear. The purpose was defined. The expectations were known. But now I was stepping into a season with no roadmap, and no guarantee of what the next chapter would look like.

I had built my leadership inside systems that demanded precision and excellence. Now God was leading me into environments where my influence would no longer come from authority but from authenticity. He was shifting my voice from operational leadership to transformational leadership. From leading missions to leading people through healing, purpose, and renewal. It was a transition I did not fully expect, yet one I could not resist. It was shaping me into the person I was meant to become beyond the role I had mastered.

Transition teaches you to listen.

To slow down.

To realign your spirit.

To reexamine your priorities.

To separate identity from assignment.

To let God interrupt your plans so He can reveal His own.

When I looked at my life through that lens, I saw transition differently. I began to realize that God was not removing stability. He was expanding it. He was not taking away purpose. He was deepening it. He was not ending influence. He was redirecting it toward places where people were waiting for what I carried.

Transition became less about loss and more about positioning.

You may be standing in your own transition right now. You may feel the distance between who you were and who you are becoming. You may feel the discomfort of old dreams dissolving or the uncertainty of new ones forming. You may be stepping out of a role that once defined you or into a calling that intimidates you.

Do not fear this season. God does His greatest shaping when your life feels unsettled.

Leadership in transition requires patience, humility, and spiritual awareness. It requires the courage to grieve old seasons without idolizing them. It requires the discipline to stand still long enough for God to speak. It requires the maturity to recognize when a door is closing not because you failed, but because you have outgrown what is behind it. And it requires the confidence to follow God into what your spirit knows before your mind understands.

This season is not about proving yourself. It is about preparing yourself.

Transition teaches you to release the identity that once served you so you can step into the identity that will serve others. It reveals strengths you did not know you had. It exposes weaknesses you can no longer ignore. It awakens purpose that has been resting beneath the surface. And it shifts your focus from achievement to assignment.

Transition is not the destruction of your identity. It is the unveiling of it.

When you walk through transition with alignment, something powerful happens. You begin to see with clarity. You begin to make decisions from purpose instead of pressure. You begin to create environments that reflect your spiritual maturity. You begin to lead with humility instead of fear. You begin to move with intention instead of reaction. You begin to operate in calling instead of comfort.

This is how leaders grow beyond achievement.

This is how leaders step into assignment.

This is how you SEE what God is doing, UNDERSTAND why He is shifting you, and MANIFEST obedience in the middle of uncertainty.

This is how leaders become the sum.

Chapter 19 SUM IT UP

THE SUM FRAMEWORK: SEE + UNDERSTAND + MANIFEST

Calling gets louder when you're ready to hear it.

SEE: the direction God is pulling you.

UNDERSTAND: what scares you about it.

MANIFEST: purpose through commitment.

BECOMING THE SUM:

1. What calling are you becoming aware of?

2. What fear stands in the way?

3. What step shows you are ready?

THE SUM CHALLENGE:

Say yes to one part of your calling.

PRAYER FOR THE JOURNEY:

God, make my calling clear and help me walk in it boldly. Amen.

"The future is shaped by the version of you that refuses to stay the same."

CHAPTER 20

BECOMING THE PERSON THE FUTURE NEEDS

Every generation is shaped by a small number of people who decide that their growth will not end with them. People who understand that maturity is not a finish line. It is preparation. People who rise because they hear a quiet pull inside them that says you were created for more than your comfort. People who understand that the future is not something you walk into. It is something you build with intention, conviction, and faith.

The world does not simply change because someone has talent. It changes because someone becomes aware of who they are called to be. It changes because someone chooses courage over familiarity, responsibility over convenience, and alignment over applause. It changes because someone steps into the identity the future requires of them, not the identity their past conditioned them to maintain.

There is a point in every leader's journey where growth becomes non-negotiable. Not because you want recognition, but because the world around you begins to reveal a need you can no longer ignore. You sense it in conversations. You sense it in the people who cross your path. You sense it in the tension between who you were and who you can feel yourself becoming. You sense it in the quiet conviction that God has placed more inside you than what you have revealed so far.

This is the moment where purpose becomes direction.

Becoming the person the future needs is not about abandoning who you are. It is about expanding who you are. It is about strengthening the parts of yourself that were once underdeveloped. It is about walking with a level of discipline, wisdom, and spiritual grounding that prepares you for assignments you cannot fully see yet.

Leadership requires a version of you that is willing to grow beyond your history.

There were many seasons in my life where I thought becoming better was simply about performance.

Discipline.

Standards.

Precision.

And while those things matter deeply, they do not build the type of leader who shapes the future. Performance builds skill. Identity builds impact. Alignment builds legacy.

The person the future needs emerges when you begin to understand that your growth is a responsibility, not a preference. You are not becoming stronger just for yourself. You are becoming stronger for the people who will depend on you. For the environments you will shape. For the conversations you will lead. For the breakthroughs you will influence. For the lives that will be connected to your presence.

People often underestimate the power of their own transformation. They assume growth is personal, but it is much bigger than that. Building yourself builds others. Healing yourself brings clarity to others. Strengthening your character stabilizes others. Walking in your calling inspires others. Your transformation is a form of service. It prepares you to carry the weight of leadership in a world that desperately needs steadiness, compassion, courage, and vision.

Becoming the person the future needs requires you to understand the season you are in. Some seasons are for healing. Some are for preparation. Some are for building. Some are for repositioning. Some are for creating. And some are for leading in ways you did not expect.

You cannot step into the next chapter of your purpose using the habits of the last chapter of your survival.

The future requires greater clarity, deeper faith, stronger discipline, and a more anchored identity. It requires you to walk with emotional maturity, spiritual awareness, and consistent integrity. It requires you to see beyond your personal preferences and into the needs of the people assigned to your influence.

This is why alignment matters so deeply. Without alignment, opportunity becomes overwhelming. Without alignment, pressure becomes destructive. Without alignment, success becomes distracting. Alignment is the foundation that allows you to carry influence without losing yourself in the process. It allows you to see clearly when the world becomes noisy. It allows you to keep God at the center of your decisions when circumstances try to pull you off course.

Leadership in the future will not belong to the strongest or the smartest. It will belong to the most aligned. The most grounded. The most disciplined. The most spiritually anchored. The ones who know how to listen, how to steady a room, how to speak life, how to discern direction, and how to build environments that bring out the best in others.

The future needs leaders willing to rise not for recognition but for responsibility.

You may not feel ready for this. Most people do not. But readiness is not the requirement. Willingness is. You become the person the future needs by showing up with intention even when you feel uncertain. You grow by allowing God to shape you. You rise by refusing to stay bound to old versions of yourself. You become the sum by walking with conviction instead of waiting for clarity.

Everything you have lived through has prepared you for the leader you are becoming right now. Your pain refined you. Your struggles strengthened you. Your victories clarified you. Your responsibilities matured you. Your calling steadied you. Your faith anchored you. Your identity is unfolding into its purpose.

The world does not need another person hiding their purpose. The world needs the version of you that is disciplined, healed, aligned, courageous, spiritually grounded, and committed to building something meaningful. The world needs the version of you that understands influence is sacred. The world needs the version of you that refuses to shrink. The world needs the version of you that carries compassion, strength, wisdom, and conviction everywhere you go.

This is the beginning of your next transformation.

This is the moment where purpose becomes leadership.

This is how you become the person the future needs.

This is how you SEE what the future is asking of you, UNDERSTAND the cost of becoming that person, and MANIFEST it through daily choices.

This is how you continue becoming the sum.

Chapter 20 SUM IT UP

THE SUM FRAMEWORK: SEE + UNDERSTAND + MANIFEST

Legacy begins with daily choices, not big moments.

SEE: what your choices are producing.

UNDERSTAND: how they shape your future.

MANIFEST: maturity by choosing with intention.

BECOMING THE SUM:

1. What legacy are you building?

2. What choices support or weaken it?

3. What aligned action can you take today?

THE SUM CHALLENGE:

Make one choice that builds your future, not your past.

PRAYER FOR THE JOURNEY:

God, guide my decisions and help me build a legacy that honors You. Amen.

"The in-between is the space where leaders are tested and revealed."

CHAPTER 21

LEADING IN THE SPACE BETWEEN WHO YOU WERE AND WHO YOU ARE BECOMING

There is a point in every journey where the old version of you has already outgrown its usefulness, but the new version of you has not fully arrived. It is an in-between space. A quiet tension. A place where confidence and uncertainty coexist. This space is uncomfortable, but it is holy. It is the space where God does His deepest work.

You cannot rush this place.

You cannot skip this place.

You cannot escape this place.

You can only grow through it.

This is the space where your identity begins to mature.

Where your purpose begins to clarify.

Where your leadership begins to shape itself around the weight of your calling.

Most people never step into who they are meant to be because they try to avoid this exact season. They want clarity before commitment. They want confirmation before courage. They want visibility before obedience. But transformation does not follow that sequence. You step first. Then the ground settles beneath your feet.

The space between who you were and who you are becoming is where your character is refined. It is where you learn to make decisions based on alignment rather than approval. It is where you discover that your voice carries authority. It is where you learn to lead without waiting for permission.

What makes this season powerful is not the absence of uncertainty. It is the presence of intentionality. When you choose to grow with purpose even when you cannot see the entire path, God begins to develop the spiritual muscle you will need for the assignments ahead. He reveals lessons you could not learn in comfort. He fortifies disciplines you could not build in ease. He stretches capacities you did not know you had.

Your life will have many in-between seasons.

Times where you feel the tension of being called forward but not fully prepared.

Times where you outgrow environments that once felt secure.

Times where God moves quietly, rearranging things in the background.

Times where your calling becomes heavier but the instructions become simpler.

This space will test your patience.

It will test your obedience.

It will test your identity.

It will test your belief in what God has planted inside you.

But this is also the space where new strength takes root.

There have been seasons in my life when I did not feel ready for what was coming next, but I could feel the pull of it. The environment felt too small. The routines felt too familiar. The comfort felt too limiting. I knew God was preparing me for something larger than the life I was living. Yet the specifics were hidden.

I had to learn how to move even when I did not feel certain.

I had to learn how to trust even when I did not see progress.

I had to learn how to step forward when standing still felt safer.

Every transition demanded more of me. More maturity. More discipline. More obedience. More alignment with my purpose. More courage to let go of things I had outgrown. These seasons revealed what no moment of clarity could. They showed me that leadership is not what you do when everything is clear. Leadership is who you are when you are still becoming.

This space between who you were and who you are becoming is also where responsibility expands.

You begin to feel accountable for more than your comfort.

You begin to feel responsible for the people God has assigned to your influence.

You begin to carry vision that stretches beyond your current environment.

You begin to operate with the understanding that your growth is no longer optional.

This is where leadership shifts from internal development to outward purpose.

You begin to recognize the needs around you.

You begin to sense which environments are waiting for your presence.

You begin to understand the urgency of becoming whole, disciplined, and spiritually grounded.

Because somewhere, someone is waiting on the leader you are becoming.

People are depending on your clarity.

People are depending on your courage.

People are depending on your healing.

People are depending on your discipline.

People are depending on your alignment with God.

People are depending on your willingness to grow beyond the limits of who you used to be.

The voice of your future begins to speak louder than the echo of your past.

When you stand in this in-between space long enough, something begins to shift. You start recognizing that the discomfort you feel is not a setback. It is a signal. It is God adjusting you. Strengthening you. Positioning you. Preparing you.

And reminding you that you are stepping into a life that requires the full version of who you are.

To lead in this space is to walk with both humility and expectation.

Humility to acknowledge what you still need to grow.

Expectation to know that what God has prepared cannot be withheld.

Humility to surrender what no longer serves you.

Expectation to step into assignments that are greater than the ones behind you.

This space is not a pause.

It is a preparation.

It is not a delay.

It is a development.

It is not a setback.

It is a set-up for the next chapter of purpose.

What you do in this space determines the strength of the leader you become.

This season is not the end of who you were.

It is the beginning of who you are becoming.

It is the bridge between identity and purpose.

It is the threshold between survival and calling.

It is the space where leadership is no longer theoretical.

It becomes the way you live.

And as you emerge from this chapter, you step forward not as the version of yourself shaped by yesterday, but as the version shaped for tomorrow.

You are stepping into the future with clarity.

You are stepping into purpose with intention.

You are stepping into leadership with identity.

You are stepping into calling with maturity.

You are stepping forward as the sum of everything God has strengthened inside you.

You have learned to SEE the season you are in, UNDERSTAND what is forming in you, and MANIFEST faithfulness right where you stand.

Chapter 21 SUM IT UP

THE SUM FRAMEWORK: SEE + UNDERSTAND + MANIFEST

Leadership starts long before anyone notices you.

SEE: your influence, even in quiet moments.

UNDERSTAND: how your character shapes your leadership.

MANIFEST: excellence in every space you walk into.

BECOMING THE SUM:

1. How do you lead without realizing it?

2. What part of your leadership needs strengthening?

3. What action will reflect excellence today?

THE SUM CHALLENGE:

Lead yourself well today.

PRAYER FOR THE JOURNEY:

God, strengthen my leadership and align my influence with purpose. Amen.

PART III

THE BECOMING

"Activation begins when your potential and your purpose finally meet."

CHAPTER 22

THE ACTIVATION OF BECOMING

There comes a moment in every person's life when excuses can no longer survive. A moment when the story you tell yourself about who you are and what you are capable of finally collides with the truth. A moment when you realize you can keep living from your wounds, or you can start living from your assignment. But you cannot do both.

If you have made it to this chapter, then you are standing at that exact moment. You have faced your story, examined your pain, confronted your patterns, and acknowledged the parts of yourself you spent years avoiding. That alone separates you from most people. But it is not enough. Healing opens the door. Purpose reveals the path. But activation is the step you must take on your own.

This is the place where becoming demands sacrifice.

When you grow, your environment must grow with you. When you heal, your habits must heal too. When you rise, the people around you must either rise with you or release you.

And when God elevates your identity, everything that is misaligned will become uncomfortable, unstable, or unsustainable.

Most people never step into who they were created to be because they refuse to let go of who they were comfortable being.

Activation requires separation.

Not emotional distance, but spiritual clarity.

Not arrogance, but awareness.

Not isolation, but intentional protection of your becoming.

There was a season of my life when I finally understood this truth. My heart wanted to grow, but everything around me kept pulling me back into who I used to be. Conversations that were rooted in negativity. Relationships that fed my insecurities. Environments that normalized small thinking. Habits that numbed instead of nurtured. People who disguised discouragement as concern. I had to decide if I wanted a comforting environment or a transforming one. I could not have both.

So I made decisions no one saw, but everyone eventually felt.

I cut off social media for five years. Because it became a doorway to comparison, noise, and distraction that I could not afford while rebuilding myself. I cut off relationships that were cutting off my growth. I stopped letting people use my life as a place to vent without also becoming a place to grow. I stopped letting negative thoughts have unlimited access to my mind. And I began forcing a new discipline into my inner world.

Every morning: a mantra.

Every day: a devotional.

Every week: intentional learning.

Every decision: alignment over approval.

Over time, my entire mindset changed. My focus sharpened. My identity strengthened. And the chaos in my life began to lose its influence because my environment no longer fed it.

But I want you to hear something clearly:

I did not become better because life got easier.

I became better because I stopped giving easy things permission to lead my life.

And now you must ask yourself the same questions I did.

What thoughts are weakening you?

What habits are stealing your clarity?

Who is speaking into your life that has no business shaping your future?

What environments are shrinking you?

What do you need to disconnect from so you can reconnect to purpose?

Growth does not happen by accident.

It happens by elimination.

It happens by pruning.

It happens by starving the things that drain you and feeding the things that build you.

This is where leaders are separated from followers. Followers wait for the environment to feel right before they change. Leaders create the environment required for transformation. Leaders adjust their inputs, boundaries, and habits to match the weight of their assignment. Leaders understand that becoming the sum means living like someone whose purpose is too valuable to be contaminated by mediocrity.

If you want peace, you must remove what disrupts it.

If you want clarity, you must silence what confuses it.

If you want discipline, you must design what supports it.

If you want purpose, you must eliminate what distracts from it.

This is the activation of becoming the sum.

You cannot walk into your future while clinging to the familiar.

You cannot carry a calling with hands still full of comfort.

You cannot be who you are meant to be while protecting who you used to be.

The world will not change because you read this book.

Your life will change because you finally decided to change how you live.

And that decision begins with the hardest truth of all:

Purpose requires sacrifice.

You may need to cut off old conversations.

You may need to limit access to certain people.

You may need to detox your mind from negativity.

You may need to delete some apps, restructure your schedule, or choose solitude instead of noise.

You may need to let go of validation, comparison, and the comfort of being understood.

Whatever it requires, honor it.

God does not elevate what you refuse to activate.

Before you move to the next chapter, I want you to take an honest pause and answer this question with the fullness of your truth:

What must die in your life so that your purpose can finally live?

Your activation begins there.

Your becoming begins there.

Your transformation takes root there.

And as you step forward into the leader you are designed to be, remember this truth woven through every chapter of this book:

To become the sum, you must protect what is becoming.

Chapter 22 SUM IT UP

THE SUM FRAMEWORK: SEE + UNDERSTAND + MANIFEST

The deeper you grow, the clearer your life becomes. Inner alignment creates outer direction.

SEE: the clarity rising inside you.

UNDERSTAND: how alignment strengthens your decisions, confidence, and leadership.

MANIFEST: purpose by moving with certainty instead of hesitation.

BECOMING THE SUM:

1. What truth about yourself is becoming clearer?

2. How is this clarity shaping the leader you are becoming?

3. What aligned step confirms your growth?

THE SUM CHALLENGE:

Make one decision today that reflects your growth, not your past.

PRAYER FOR THE JOURNEY:

God, align my heart, mind, and purpose. Strengthen my clarity and let my steps honor the leader You are shaping in me. Amen.

"Becoming the sum is a discipline you practice daily."

CHAPTER 23

THE DISCIPLINE OF BECOMING

Activation sparks the beginning of change, but consistency determines whether it lasts. The truth that many people avoid is that breakthroughs are easy compared to what comes next. Anyone can have a moment of clarity, courage, or conviction. Anyone can experience a shift in their thinking or feel a surge of motivation after reading something powerful. But transformation is not built on moments. It is built on behaviors. It is built on daily choices that reinforce who you are becoming long after the emotion of the moment fades.

Purpose requires stability.

Leadership requires discipline.

Growth requires systems.

Identity requires reinforcement.

You cannot build a meaningful life on occasional effort or inconsistent habits.

You must build it on patterns that support who you are becoming. Your future relies far more on what you repeat than what you occasionally feel inspired to do.

There was a time in my life when this became painfully clear. I had reached a point in my journey where I could no longer depend on emotion to carry me. Some days I woke up full of hope. Other days I woke up heavy with doubt. Some days I felt strong. Other days I felt like the same fears I thought I had defeated were waiting for me at the edge of the bed. My transformation began, but my consistency would determine whether it lasted.

So I built discipline around my life the same way someone constructs scaffolding around a structure being rebuilt. Not because I was weak, but because I knew I needed support while I was growing stronger. I created morning routines to secure my mindset. I replaced unhealthy thoughts with daily mantras and scripture. I controlled my inputs with intentional reading and devotionals. I monitored the tone of conversations around me. I removed negativity and replaced it with possibility. I made learning a lifestyle, not a task. And I surrounded myself with people who spoke life, not doubt.

None of these changes happened quickly. They happened one decision at a time. One sunrise at a time. One choice to protect my mind instead of allowing it to drift. One act of discipline that reminded me of who I was becoming instead of who I used to be. Over time, consistency became part of my character. Not perfection. Not constant motivation. Just steady, faithful effort.

This is where purpose becomes visible.

People are inspired by talent, but they trust consistency.

People follow passion, but they grow from discipline.

People admire ability, but they are transformed by reliability.

You cannot carry purpose without carrying discipline.

You cannot build influence without building habits.

You cannot lead others if you cannot lead yourself.

There is a version of you that God has called you to become. That version is not built on emotional highs. It is built on structure. It is built on small daily decisions that align your life with your calling. It is built on the quiet things no one sees. It is built on the work you do when no one is clapping. It is built on what you repeat, not what you occasionally attempt.

Many people misunderstand purpose. They think purpose is revealed in big moments. They imagine a sudden clarity or a singular calling. But purpose is not discovered in extremes. It is uncovered in consistency. It reveals itself to those who show up every day, who take the next step when no one is watching, who stay committed long after inspiration fades.

Purpose is motion, not theory.

Purpose is practice, not perfection.

Purpose is direction, not speed.

There were seasons when my purpose was visible and seasons when it was not. Only one thing stayed constant. I kept moving. Even when the way forward felt unclear, I kept moving.

Even when doubt whispered that I would fail, I kept moving. Even when life felt unfair, heavy, or discouraging, I kept moving.

Purpose is revealed through movement.

Some people never find purpose because they wait for clarity before taking action. But clarity often comes after you move, not before. When you act with discipline, identity begins to form. When identity begins to form, purpose begins to reveal itself. When purpose reveals itself, direction becomes clear. And when direction becomes clear, every step you take begins to make sense.

You may not know exactly where God is leading you.

You may not understand why certain things happened.

You may still be healing.

You may still be learning.

You may still be growing.

But your responsibility is simple: keep moving forward with consistency.

The small things matter.

The quiet things matter.

The unseen things matter.

The personal standards you set matter.

The internal discipline you choose matters.

The steps you take when you feel tired matter.

Your faithfulness when no one notices matters.

Your progress when no one applauds matters.

Because these are the things that shape character, not moments.

These are the things that shape leadership, not emotions.

These are the things that shape identity, not circumstances.

You are becoming the sum, and the sum is built one decision at a time.

Turn the page.

Let purpose move with you.

Chapter 23 SUM IT UP

THE SUM FRAMEWORK: SEE + UNDERSTAND + MANIFEST

Your journey has not been random. Every step prepared you for this level of leadership.

SEE: the evidence of God's hand throughout your life.

UNDERSTAND: how every season strengthened your character.

MANIFEST: trust by walking with confidence in the direction God is taking you.

BECOMING THE SUM:

1. Where do you see God's guidance most clearly?

2. What wisdom did past seasons give you?

3. How can you lead with more trust and less fear?

THE SUM CHALLENGE:

Identify one place where God guided you and thank Him for it today.

PRAYER FOR THE JOURNEY:

God, thank You for guiding me through every moment. Strengthen my confidence as I step into what You designed for me. Amen.

"Purpose-driven leadership disrupts everything built on comfort."

CHAPTER 24

LEADING WITH PURPOSE IN A WORLD THAT RESISTS IT

There is a reason so few people ever step fully into their purpose. It is not because they lack talent or desire. It is because the moment you begin to live with intention, everything around you will test whether you are serious. Purpose is beautiful when imagined, but difficult when lived. It asks you to carry yourself differently in a world that benefits from you staying the same. It requires courage that cannot be borrowed, confidence that must be built, and consistency that must be earned.

Purpose will always put you at odds with the environments that shaped your old identity. People who were comfortable with the older version of you may not understand the disciplined, focused, intentional version you are becoming. Circumstances that once felt familiar may begin to feel limiting. Conversations that used to entertain you may now disrupt your peace. The more clearly you see who you are meant to become, the more uncomfortable you will feel in spaces where you once fit easily.

This discomfort is not a sign you are lost. It is a sign you are growing.

The moment purpose is activated, your life will begin to make a new kind of demand. You will feel the pull to align everything you do with who you are becoming. Your schedule will need structure. Your habits will need reinforcement. Your relationships will require discernment. Your time, energy, and attention will need protecting in ways they never did before.

Leadership is about living in a way that pulls people higher simply by being who you are. But to live at that level, you must be willing to stand firm when your surroundings try to pull you back. Every meaningful leader, in any field or calling, has had to make peace with the reality that purpose sometimes feels lonely. Growth sometimes feels misunderstood. And elevation always requires separation.

You will know you are elevating when silence becomes more nourishing than noise. When your time becomes more valuable than your comfort. When your goals matter more than the opinions of people who do not carry your vision. When your peace speaks louder than your insecurities. When the future matters more than the familiarity of the past.

Life will not always affirm your direction. People will not always celebrate your progress. The world will not always understand your calling. Leadership requires that you stay aligned even when external validation is silent. Because purpose is not proven by applause. Purpose is proven by persistence. It is proven by the decisions you make when the cost becomes real.

I spent years learning this truth. There were moments in my career when purpose placed weight on my shoulders that I did not feel ready to carry. Moments when serving others required more sacrifice than I anticipated. Moments when I had to stand firm in my calling even when I felt isolated or unseen. I watched communities collapse under the weight of hopelessness, students cry out for direction, teammates carry invisible pain, service members lose battles in their mind long before they lost them in the field. These experiences strengthened my dependence on God and sharpened my understanding of leadership. They taught me that purpose is not about position. It is about service. It is about recognizing the weight of the world that rests in front of you and choosing to lift it anyway.

You may not realize it now, but someone is depending on you to stay committed to your growth. Someone will need your strength. Someone will need your kindness. Someone will need your voice, your story, your example, your courage, and your consistency. You may never know their name, but your purpose will reach them all the same.

This is what separates leadership from influence. Influence is what you get from people. Leadership is what you give to people.

Purpose in motion is not measured in titles or recognition. It is measured in who becomes stronger because you refused to give up. It is measured in the people who feel seen because you grew in empathy. It is measured in the lives redirected because you lived with integrity. It is measured in the difference you make quietly, humbly, and consistently.

Because becoming the sum means carrying your purpose into every room, every conversation, every challenge, and every opportunity. Not with perfection, but with devotion. Not with ego, but with alignment. Not with force, but with clarity.

Your life is not an accident. Your purpose is not optional. And your leadership is not for you alone.

Turn the page.

There is more becoming the sum ahead.

Chapter 24 SUM IT UP

THE SUM FRAMEWORK: SEE + UNDERSTAND + MANIFEST

Real leadership starts when you stop striving to be perfect and start standing in truth.

SEE: where perfection has held you back.

UNDERSTAND: how authenticity deepens your influence.

MANIFEST: truth by showing up as the leader you already are.

BECOMING THE SUM:

1. Where have you overworked yourself trying to be perfect?

2. How would your life change if you chose truth instead?

3. What honest step can you take today?

THE SUM CHALLENGE:

Show up as your true self in one space where you've been performing.

PRAYER FOR THE JOURNEY:

God, free me from perfection and help me walk boldly in authenticity and truth. Amen.

"Influence is a weight and impact is a gift. You must learn to carry both."

CHAPTER 25

THE WEIGHT OF INFLUENCE AND THE GIFT OF IMPACT

There comes a point in becoming the sum where you realize leadership is about what you release into the world. It becomes about the lives touched, the people strengthened, the hope restored, and the futures reshaped because you made a decision to live with intention. Leadership stops being a personal climb and becomes a responsibility you carry with honor.

The weight of influence is real.

And the weight of impact is sacred.

Most people underestimate how deeply their decisions echo beyond their own life. They underestimate how a single act of integrity might protect someone else's faith. How a moment of kindness might interrupt someone's despair. How a word of encouragement might become the turning point of someone's story. How a consistent example might become the anchor someone else holds onto while fighting silent battles.

When you begin to live with purpose, you stop asking questions like "What do I get from this?" and start asking "Who becomes stronger because I showed up today?"

This is the shift from achievement to assignment.

Purpose stops being a personal pursuit and becomes a calling to create change wherever your presence is placed. Leadership becomes the process of lifting the world around you by standing fully in who God created you to be.

But here is something that most leaders never admit.

The deeper your calling, the heavier the responsibility feels.

There will be days when your influence stretches you. Days when people look to you for strength you do not think you have. Days when you must make decisions that are not easy, convenient, or comfortable. Days when you carry the emotional weight of those who trust you. Days when you must lead with grace even when your own heart is weary.

This is not weakness.

This is leadership.

I have felt this weight many times across my life and career.

Standing in classrooms where students searched for purpose without knowing how to name their pain.

Facing hallways in juvenile detention centers where young boys begged for belonging in places that were never meant to become their home.

Watching teammates in Special Operations carry trauma that no one else could see because the uniform demanded silence.

Speaking to leaders who were exhausted from pouring into others without receiving anything back.

Hearing the voices of people navigating hardships they never imagined.

Mourning friends who left this world too early because they believed no one would understand the battles in their mind.

These moments forced me to grow spiritually, emotionally, and mentally. They forced me to build capacity. They forced me to elevate my own discipline so that others could stand on the strength I gained. They forced me to mature in ways I did not expect and lead in places I never imagined.

Influence is not a privilege.

It is a responsibility.

People are not drawn to your perfection.

They are drawn to your consistency.

They are drawn to your authenticity.

They are drawn to the way you rise after breaking.

They are drawn to the truth in your voice and the conviction in your steps.

They are drawn to the light you carry because it reminds them of their own.

That is impact.

And when your leadership becomes rooted in identity instead of image, something powerful happens. You begin to carry influence without fear. You begin to navigate challenges without losing yourself. You begin to serve without needing recognition. You begin to walk into uncertainty with clarity. You begin to speak life where others speak doubt, and you begin to stand in places others would have collapsed.

Leadership is not about being the strongest or most intelligent person in the room.

It is about being the most grounded.

The most self-aware.

The most aligned.

The most committed.

The most faithful to the assignment God placed inside you.

Some people will never say thank you.

Some people will never understand the sacrifice.

Some people will never recognize the weight you carry.

That is not why you lead.

You lead because someone once led you.

You lead because God entrusted you with influence.

You lead because your story carries healing for someone else.

You lead because your obedience opens doors others cannot open for themselves.

You lead because impact is not about applause.

Impact is about transformation.

Think about your family.

Think about your community.

Think about the people watching you from a distance.

Think about the ones you have not met yet.

Your impact is already unfolding.

Your influence is already growing.

Your purpose is already at work.

Carry it well.

Carry it with grace.

Carry it with courage.

Carry it with humility.

Carry it with the awareness that leadership is a gift and your life is planting seeds you may never see bloom.

Turn the page.

You are stepping deeper into the life you were born to lead.

Chapter 25 SUM IT UP

THE SUM FRAMEWORK: SEE + UNDERSTAND + MANIFEST

To elevate, you must release what no longer aligns with your calling.

SEE: the relationships, habits, or mindsets that no longer support your growth.

UNDERSTAND: how holding onto them limits your future.

MANIFEST: courage by releasing anything that cannot go with you to the next level.

BECOMING THE SUM:

1. What are you still holding onto that holds you back?

2. Why has it been hard to let go?

3. What can you release today?

THE SUM CHALLENGE:

Let go of one misaligned thing that no longer belongs.

PRAYER FOR THE JOURNEY:

God, give me strength to release what no longer aligns with my calling. Prepare me for what is ahead. Amen.

"The future belongs to the leaders willing to build what does not yet exist."

CHAPTER 26

THE LEADER WHO BUILDS THE FUTURE

There comes a moment in every leader's journey when you realize the greatest measure of your growth is what your growth makes possible in others. Influence stops being about your direction alone and becomes about the direction you help others discover. It is the moment when your life shifts from developing your potential to unlocking the potential of the people entrusted to your path. Leadership no longer becomes a reflection of who you are becoming, but a catalyst for who others are capable of becoming because of your presence.

This shift happens when you start seeing leadership as something larger than achievement. It happens when your confidence is no longer fragile, when your identity is no longer performance based, and when your purpose is no longer something you protect, but something you share. You begin to understand that the world will be shaped just as much by the strength of the people you elevate as by the results you achieve personally.

Leadership matures when your life becomes fertile ground for the growth of others.

I have seen this truth unfold in many seasons. In classrooms where students carried more pain than guidance. In detention centers where children needed someone to believe they could rise beyond the boundaries placed around them. In formations where Soldiers battled invisible wars. In conversations with employees, parents, teachers, leaders, and young people trying to find their place in a world that often misunderstands them. These moments taught me that people do not rise because you tell them to. They rise because someone makes room for their potential to breathe.

And that room is created through example, presence, and genuine belief.

When you begin to live aligned with your purpose, your life naturally creates space for others to grow. This is through invitation. Through authenticity. Through embodiment. People feel safer to stretch when they see someone else living fully in their calling. They feel permission to become more when they watch you refuse to shrink.

Leadership that builds leaders is not loud. It is steady. It listens deeply. It observes patterns no one else sees. It recognizes potential before it is obvious. It cares enough to guide without controlling. It encourages without rescuing. It challenges without shaming. It lifts without lifting itself.

This kind of leadership does not create followers.

It creates futures.

And when you begin to build others, something powerful happens inside you. Your purpose expands. Your vision expands. Your sense of responsibility expands. You start to understand that God entrusts growth to those who steward influence with humility and care. You begin to feel the weight of impact in a new way, not as a burden, but as an honor.

Because leadership is not about becoming impressive.

It is about becoming useful.

This chapter is the transition where your influence begins to multiply. This is where the life you are becoming steps into alignment with the future you are meant to shape. You are no longer growing only for yourself. You are growing for the people who will learn from your strength, find clarity through your example, and discover purpose through your presence.

The life in front of you requires a specific kind of leader.

A leader who is grounded enough to grow others.

A leader who is courageous enough to speak truth with compassion.

A leader who is disciplined enough to remain consistent.

A leader who is humble enough to keep learning.

A leader who is spiritually aligned enough to hear God clearly.

A leader who is emotionally mature enough to guide without controlling.

A leader who is strong enough to carry influence without losing identity.

You becoming the sum is meant to extend through you.

There is someone in your life right now who is watching how you move. Someone who is looking for an example of how to lead with integrity. Someone who is searching for a reason to believe they can change. Someone who needs the kind of encouragement you once needed. Someone who will become stronger because you committed to rising. Someone whose future hinges on your willingness to show up with purpose.

You may not know their name yet.

You may not recognize them when they appear.

You may not realize the depth of your impact in their life until years later. But your leadership is already shaping them.

That is the reality of influence.

That is the responsibility of growth.

That is the calling of becoming the sum.

Your leadership is not an idea.

It is a foundation for someone else's future.

Turn the page.

You are becoming the leader who builds lives, legacies, and the future.

Chapter 26 SUM IT UP

THE SUM FRAMEWORK: SEE + UNDERSTAND + MANIFEST

You are standing in strength you once prayed for. Walk in the wholeness God built in you.

SEE: the moments that made you question your worth.

UNDERSTAND: how those moments strengthened your identity.

MANIFEST: confidence by stepping into the whole version of yourself.

BECOMING THE SUM:

1. What experience made you doubt your value?

2. How did it build strength in you?

3. What does walking in wholeness look like today?

THE SUM CHALLENGE:

Act today from your wholeness, not your wounds.

PRAYER FOR THE JOURNEY:

God, thank You for restoring me. Help me walk in the strength You shaped through every season. Amen.

"Your greatest strength is the stability you build within."

CHAPTER 27

THE INNER FORTRESS OF A LEADER

There is a part of leadership that happens in public, where the world can see the outcomes of your growth. But the truest, most enduring part of leadership is built in private. It is formed in the quiet moments no one congratulates you for. It is strengthened in the discipline that no one notices. It is shaped in the battles you fight without an audience. It is refined in the decisions you make when you are tired, stretched, or unseen. This is the inner fortress of a leader, and without it, nothing you build externally will last.

Every leader eventually reaches a point where success, influence, or momentum is not enough to sustain them. The outer life rises only as high as the inner life allows. This is where many people falter. They pursue growth but neglect the structure required to protect it. They seek purpose but overlook the emotional and spiritual foundation needed to carry it. They desire impact but ignore the internal habits that make impact sustainable.

Leadership is built from the inside out.

Your mind, your spirit, your emotional health, your discipline, your self-awareness, and your relationship with God all create the internal conditions that support your external influence. If these inner structures are weak, life will expose the cracks. If these structures are strong, nothing you face will collapse you.

I learned this truth through years of leading in environments where external chaos was constant. There were seasons when everything around me was unpredictable. Missions where danger was always present. Workplaces where pressure never eased. Homes where responsibility stretched beyond capacity. Communities where trauma lived beneath the surface. I saw quickly that skill was not enough. Talent was not enough. Performance was not enough. Even courage was not enough.

The leaders who lasted were the ones who cultivated their inner world.

They were disciplined when no one monitored them.

They were grounded when circumstances shook others.

They were clear when confusion surrounded them.

They were steady when emotions ran high.

They were centered when pressure intensified.

They were spiritually aligned when others depended solely on willpower.

These leaders built something inside themselves that could not be taken away by stress, noise, or hardship. They didn't lead from adrenaline. They led from foundation.

And the same is required for you.

Your inner world is not a side project. It is the core of everything you will create. It determines how you think, react, communicate, decide, love, speak, and endure. It shapes your patience, compassion, clarity, and leadership presence. It is the anchor when life challenges your confidence. It is the compass when you feel lost. It is the stabilizer when people depend on you. It is the sanctuary where God refines you. And it is the vault where your purpose is stored.

Some people spend their entire lives strengthening their image and neglecting their identity. They build resumes but not resilience. They build influence but not integrity. They build networks but not emotional maturity. They build opportunities but not character. Eventually life reveals the truth. Your gift can open doors, but only your inner world can keep them open.

The inner fortress is not built by accident. It is built through discipline. It is built through prayer and reflection. It is built through honest self-evaluation. It is built by aligning your thoughts with truth instead of fear. It is built by confronting the parts of you that sabotage growth. It is built by choosing peace over impulse and clarity over chaos.

It is built one decision at a time.

The stronger your inner world becomes, the more predictable your leadership becomes. Life doesn't get easier, but your response becomes anchored. You become someone who does not crumble at the first sign of pressure. You become someone who leads with patience when others react. You become someone who does not need constant reassurance to remain grounded. You become someone who can see beyond the moment because your emotions stay tethered to truth rather than insecurity.

Your inner world becomes the environment where your calling matures.

And you cannot pour into others if your internal reservoir is empty. You cannot guide people with clarity if your thoughts remain scattered. You cannot lift others if everything inside you is collapsing under quiet weight. You cannot walk in purpose if your mind is still rehearsing your past. You cannot teach strength if your spirit is unstable. You cannot become the sum if your internal world is still fragmented.

This chapter is an invitation to build the foundation that will carry the rest of your life.

Your external impact will only grow as far as your internal world allows.

Your becoming will only rise as high as your foundation is strong.

The leadership you carry will only endure as long as your inner world is protected.

Turn the page.

Your foundation is forming.

Your journey of becoming the sum continues.

Chapter 27 SUM IT UP

THE SUM FRAMEWORK: SEE + UNDERSTAND + MANIFEST

Your future cannot be built on the version of you that life tried to keep small.

SEE: the ways your past still influences your decisions.

UNDERSTAND: why certain patterns still try to pull you back.

MANIFEST: freedom by choosing a future aligned with your identity.

BECOMING THE SUM:

1. What old pattern still shows up?

2. Why does it feel familiar?

3. What freedom action can you take today?

THE SUM CHALLENGE:

Choose one action that represents your future instead of your past.

PRAYER FOR THE JOURNEY:

God, release me from old versions of myself and guide me into the future You designed for me. Amen.

"Calling prepares you long before the future arrives."

CHAPTER 28

THE FUTURE YOU ARE CALLED TO LEAD

Every season of growth brings you to a crossroads where you must decide whether you will simply continue becoming, or whether you will begin directing your becoming with intention. The shift from healing to building, from growth to direction, is one of the most powerful transitions a leader can make. It is the point where you stop surviving the life you have lived and start architecting the life you are called to lead.

Many people evolve without ever embracing this moment. They change, but they do not guide their change. They mature, but they do not channel their maturity. They heal, but they do not build from that healing. They improve, but they do not take hold of the clarity that improvement creates. And so their transformation remains incomplete because it never receives direction.

Leadership requires direction.

You cannot walk into your calling passively. You cannot drift into purpose. You cannot silently hope a meaningful future shows up on its own.

You must shape the life you are becoming with clarity, intention, obedience, and long-term conviction. You must decide that your future requires more from you than your past ever demanded. You must recognize that your growth is not only preparing you for what is ahead but it is asking you to participate in the building of what is ahead.

What does that look like?

It begins with vision.

Not the vision others place on you, but the vision God formed in you.

Not the expectations you inherited, but the assignment you were created for.

Vision is not a picture of the life you want. It is the picture of the life that wants you. The one your gifts testify to, your spirit leans toward, and your purpose keeps pointing back to even when you try to ignore it. Vision does not bargain. It calls. It nudges. It interrupts. It whispers. It follows you into every room, every season, every transition, and every prayer. It waits for you to stop shrinking long enough to acknowledge that you were built for more than surviving the days you have already lived.

Vision is not loud, but it is persistent.

Some of your greatest clarity comes in seasons when life feels uncertain. The moment you feel stripped of what is familiar is often the moment purpose becomes easier to hear. When noise quiets, the voice of your spirit rises. When distractions fall away, direction becomes clearer. When you are no longer held in place by people's expectations, you finally have the space to consider God's.

That is where I found myself years into my journey. After surviving trauma, deployments, losses, restarts, setbacks, and redirections, my life reached a point where responsibility was no longer enough. Performance was no longer enough. Achievement was no longer enough. Titles were no longer enough. I needed clarity about where my journey was leading me.

And what I learned is this:

Your purpose becomes visible when you stop negotiating with who you used to be.

Your calling becomes accessible when you stop hiding the parts of your story that shaped your compassion, your conviction, and your authority. Your vision becomes powerful when you stop trying to fit into environments that cannot sustain the person you are becoming. Spiritual alignment becomes natural when you stop relying on strength alone and allow God to stretch, strengthen, and position you.

This is where the future enters.

The life you are called to lead is not built on what you've lost, but on what you carry. It is shaped by your empathy, sharpened by your discipline, purified by your healing, fueled by your faith, and guided by the lessons you refused to let destroy you. The future version of you is not waiting on more time, more resources, or more confidence. It is waiting on your willingness to trust the person God is shaping you into.

The world you are moving toward requires:

A clearer mind.

A steadier spirit.

A stronger foundation.

A deeper conviction.

A louder courage.

A more honest self-leadership.

A wider compassion.

A greater willingness to serve.

And a heart that is aligned with God, not with fear.

It also requires discipline that matches your destiny. Not to earn the calling, but to sustain it. Not to impress others, but to remain prepared for the opportunities God places in your path. Not to perform, but to remain ready. Not to prove yourself, but to honor the doors that were opened for you long before you knew they existed.

You are being shaped for a future that needs your presence, your voice, your experience, your wisdom, and your becoming. Every environment you have navigated has prepared you for an assignment that extends beyond your personal ambition. Every hardship has forged something in you that is meant to serve others. Every chapter of your story has placed a tool in your hands that someone else will need to climb out of what is holding them back.

Leadership is not about walking toward your future alone. It is about carrying others into theirs.

Your next chapter requires the boldest version of your.

Your next season depends on the clarity you embrace today.

Your purpose is already waiting.

Your future is already forming.

Your becoming is already in motion.

Turn the page.

The leader you are becoming is stepping forward.

Chapter 28 SUM IT UP

THE SUM FRAMEWORK: SEE + UNDERSTAND + MANIFEST

Consistency builds identity. Small aligned actions determine long-term growth.

SEE: the actions that support your elevation.

UNDERSTAND: why they bring peace and clarity.

MANIFEST: consistency through daily discipline.

BECOMING THE SUM:

1. What aligned habit strengthens your growth?

2. Why is it effective?

3. How can you repeat it today?

THE SUM CHALLENGE:

Repeat one aligned habit with full intention.

PRAYER FOR THE JOURNEY:

God, strengthen my consistency and help me honor the habits that support my purpose. Amen.

"Identity becomes power when you learn to guard it with intention."

CHAPTER 29

THE IDENTITY YOU MUST PROTECT

There comes a point in every leader's journey when the work shifts from discovering who you are to protecting who you are becoming. Growth demands courage, but protection demands maturity. Identity is not something you uncover once and then own for life. Identity is something you must guard, tend to, develop, and reinforce because everything in the world will try to pull you back into a smaller version of yourself.

Most people underestimate this part of leadership. They believe the hardest battle is becoming someone new, but the truth is that becoming is only the first ascent. The real challenge begins when life, environments, expectations, and even your own habits attempt to return you to the person you learned to outgrow.

Identity needs protection because identity is fragile in its formation. You can begin healing and still slip into old self-doubt. You can start experiencing purpose and still feel the tug of familiar insecurity. You can grow beyond your past and still be tempted to repeat it. You can move into a new season and still be shadowed by the voice of who you used to be.

Growth does not eliminate resistance. It invites it.

When you start walking in confidence, someone will question your competence.

When you begin setting boundaries, someone will accuse you of changing.

When you rise above old environments, someone will try to guilt you into returning.

When you finally understand your value, someone will try to convince you it was never there.

The moment you evolve, you threaten the comfort of people who depend on the version of you that no longer exists. And this is where many leaders lose themselves, not because they are weak, but because they still care. They care about relationships. They care about belonging. They care about connection. They care about acceptance. And without realizing it, they slowly shrink to fit spaces they have already outgrown.

Every great leader faces this choice: Will you continue becoming the person your purpose requires, or return to the person your past prefers?

Identity is not only about who you are.

It is about what you refuse to return to.

I learned this in seasons when external success was rising quickly, while internal pressure grew just as fast. During my years of carrying responsibility for teams, missions, people, and outcomes that demanded precision, I found myself bending under the weight of expectations I had never experienced before. Respect grew, responsibility multiplied, and so did the silent pressure to remain everything to everyone.

But identity cannot survive when it is stretched across too many expectations. At some point you must choose the identity that aligns with your assignment rather than the identities others attach to you. There were moments when I had to step back and ask myself whether I was evolving out of conviction or performing out of obligation. Whether I was moving toward purpose or drifting toward burnout. Whether I was leading others from strength or losing myself quietly in the process.

And this is where spiritual alignment became more than belief, it became necessity.

The more leadership demanded from me, the more I needed God to anchor me. I watched my family fight battles they did not choose. I sat across from many who were searching for a reason to believe they mattered. I worked through nights so my teammates could walk into chaos with at least a thread of predictability. I stood in classrooms speaking with students who were brilliant but lost. I buried friends and a family member who chose to leave this world before their purpose could unfold.

Pain has a way of stripping you down to your true identity.

Purpose has a way of revealing who you were always meant to be.

And both require protection.

Identity must be guarded against:

Noise that distracts you.

People who drain you.

Habits that weaken you.

Thoughts that sabotage you.

Temptations that derail you.

Old versions that invite you back.

Comparison that steals your peace.

Negativity that corrodes your courage.

Opportunities that do not align with your assignment.

Your identity is the foundation of your leadership.

And any foundation left unprotected will eventually fracture.

This chapter is your call to protect the person you are becoming with the same intensity you once used to survive. To guard your mindset with discipline. To guard your heart with wisdom. To guard your energy with boundaries. To guard your purpose with intentionality. To guard your growth with maturity. To guard your spirit with humility and devotion. To guard your becoming as if your future depends on it because it does.

Your identity is not just who you are.

It is the blueprint for the leader the world needs you to become and the sum of your life every lesson, every wound, every transformation and deserves protection.

Chapter 29 SUM IT UP

THE SUM FRAMEWORK: SEE + UNDERSTAND + MANIFEST

Discomfort reveals your edges. You are stretching because you are expanding.

SEE: the discomfort rising in you.

UNDERSTAND: what it is pushing you toward.

MANIFEST: courage by stepping forward even when it feels new.

BECOMING THE SUM:

1. What discomfort is calling you to grow?

2. What truth does it reveal?

3. What step can you take today?

THE SUM CHALLENGE:

Lean into the discomfort. Move toward growth.

PRAYER FOR THE JOURNEY:

God, strengthen me to embrace growth and lead through discomfort. Amen.

"Becoming the sum demands responsibility for the life you were created to lead."

CHAPTER 30

THE RESPONSIBILITY OF BECOMING

There comes a point in your life when you stop feeling like you are waiting for a breakthrough and start realizing that the breakthrough has been waiting for you. It is not dramatic. It is not loud. It arrives in the stillness of honest reflection. You begin to see that the distance between the life you have and the life you desire is not measured in luck or timing, but in responsibility. You start recognizing the choices that strengthened you and the ones that weakened you. You notice how your habits have shaped your identity and how your thoughts have shaped your direction. In that moment, something shifts. You understand that your next level is not hidden. It is simply unclaimed.

Most people think transformation happens when circumstances change, but true transformation begins when you change your relationship with yourself. When you stop ignoring the patterns that have held you back. When you stop settling for the version of yourself that survival required. When you stop postponing the work you know you must do. Responsibility is not punishment. Responsibility is clarity. It is the realization that the person you are becoming is shaped by what you consistently allow, accept, and practice. Your future is not shaped by the moments that happen to you. It is shaped by the choices you make after those moments.

As you grow, you will notice that responsibility no longer feels like pressure. It begins to feel like alignment. You start recognizing what belongs in your life and what does not. You become more aware of the environments that empower your calling and the ones that suffocate it. You identify the conversations that elevate you and the ones that drain you. You begin to separate your identity from your old behaviors, your old thinking, and your old limitations. Responsibility becomes the moment where you choose to protect your growth rather than sabotage it.

At this point in your journey, responsibility becomes the threshold between who you were and who you are becoming. It is the point where excuses lose their appeal because your potential becomes undeniable. You can feel something rising in you, something that refuses to let you stay comfortable with who you were. Responsibility calls you to elevate your standard, refine your mindset, discipline your habits, and honor the life you were created to build. It is the moment where you realize that becoming the sum is not something you drift into. It is something you choose with intention.

Responsibility demands that you confront the thoughts that shape your internal world. Your internal dialogue carries more influence than any external criticism ever could. The way you speak to yourself becomes the environment you live in. The beliefs you reinforce create the ceiling you operate under. If you constantly tell yourself that you are overwhelmed, unqualified, or incapable, your actions will follow those beliefs. If you train your mind to think with clarity, discipline, and conviction, your leadership will reflect that posture. Responsibility asks you to take ownership of the conversations you have with yourself when no one else can hear them.

You will also find that responsibility requires you to make intentional decisions about your habits. You do not rise into your next level by accident. You rise through consistency. You rise through discipline. You rise through the standards you set for yourself when motivation fades. This may require restructuring your daily routines, strengthening your boundaries, waking up earlier, reading more, praying more, thinking more critically, or surrounding yourself with people who challenge you the way growth requires. You cannot become your future self with the habits that belonged to your former self.

Part of responsibility is learning what you must release. There will be relationships, environments, or patterns that served a purpose in a previous season but are not meant to follow you into the next. Responsibility requires you to examine what drains your focus or complicates your peace. It asks you to recognize when you have outgrown a mindset, a routine, or an identity that once felt familiar. This is not abandonment. It is alignment. It is protecting the version of you that is emerging.

Responsibility invites you to develop emotional maturity. Growth is not only measured in achievement. It is measured in how you respond to difficulty, criticism, challenge, and disappointment. Emotional maturity means choosing deeper understanding over reaction. It means regulating your emotions so your decisions come from stability rather than impulse. It means refusing to allow temporary feelings to dictate long-term direction. This level of maturity strengthens your leadership because it strengthens the foundation of who you are.

As your responsibility grows, you begin to understand that your transformation is connected to the people around you. When you elevate your standards, your relationships shift. When you grow in discipline, the people influenced by you rise as well. When you heal, you create space for others to heal. Responsibility is not isolation. Responsibility is impact. It shapes the culture of your home, your friendships, your workplace, and your community. The way you carry yourself becomes permission for others to rise. The way you lead yourself becomes instruction for those who follow you.

Responsibility does not ask you to have everything figured out. It asks you to be honest about where you currently stand and faithful to who you are becoming. It asks you to look at your life and admit where improvement is needed without fear or denial. It asks you to carry your growth with maturity and protect the identity you are building. This is where the becoming begins to stabilize. Not because life gets easier, but because you are stronger, wiser, and more disciplined in how you move through it.

Responsibility is the doorway. And the person you are becoming is waiting for you on the other side.

Chapter 30 SUM IT UP

THE SUM FRAMEWORK: SEE + UNDERSTAND + MANIFEST

Ownership is maturity. You rise when you take responsibility for your life.

SEE: what needs your ownership.

UNDERSTAND: how your choices shape your path.

MANIFEST: maturity through accountability.

BECOMING THE SUM:

1. Where do you need to take responsibility?

2. What did avoiding it cost you?

3. What corrective step can you take today?

THE SUM CHALLENGE:

Take ownership of one area you've avoided.

PRAYER FOR THE JOURNEY:

God, help me move with maturity and own the choices that shape my growth. Amen.

"Master the inner world, and the outer world loses its power over you."

CHAPTER 31

MASTERY OF THE INNER WORLD

Mastery does not begin when you achieve success. Mastery begins when you learn how to sustain the person you are becoming. Growth is only the first half of transformation. The second half is preservation. It is learning how to protect your progress, nurture your identity, and strengthen the internal world that carries everything you will become.

Many people rise for a moment.

Few rise for a lifetime.

The difference is mastery.

Mastery is not perfection nor is it flawlessness. It is not the elimination of struggle. Mastery is the commitment to develop such clarity, such discipline, and such emotional strength that your inner world remains stable even when your outer world is shifting. It is the ability to stay aligned when life becomes unpredictable. It is the maturity to lead yourself through uncertainty with conviction rather than fear.

As you grow in responsibility, you begin to recognize that your greatest battles are rarely external. The true battles happen within your thoughts, your impulses, your beliefs, your fears, your doubts, and your reactions. Mastery invites you into a deeper relationship with yourself. It asks you to examine the places where your insecurity speaks louder than your potential. It asks you to confront the voice that questions your worth, your ability, or your readiness. It asks you to build strength in the areas where your old self once had the most control.

Mastery requires stillness.

Not stillness as inactivity, but stillness as presence.

The ability to sit with your thoughts without being overwhelmed by them.

It is the ability to slow your mind long enough to examine what you are feeling and why you are feeling it. Without stillness, your emotions become louder than your intentions. Without stillness, your reactions outrun your wisdom. Without stillness, you repeat patterns you worked hard to grow past. Mastery invites you to pause long enough to recognize the difference between impulse and truth.

Mastery also demands discipline. Discipline is not about punishment. It is about direction. It keeps your mind aligned with your values and your actions aligned with your purpose. It protects your progress when motivation fades. Discipline is what builds leaders who remain consistent long after the excitement disappears. Mastery is choosing what strengthens you even when it is not convenient. It is reading when you would rather scroll. It is praying when you would rather worry. It is speaking purpose when old patterns whisper doubt. It is listening to wisdom when your emotions beg for control.

Mastery is deeply spiritual. You cannot rise into your highest potential without acknowledging the power that sustains you. Every leader reaches a point where talent is no longer enough and skill is no longer sufficient. You need grounding. You need alignment. You need truth that does not shift with your circumstances. For many people, mastery begins when they realize they cannot lead themselves without guidance from the One who shaped them. Spiritual alignment strengthens your identity. It gives you direction when the path feels unclear. It keeps your heart grounded in purpose rather than ego.

Mastery also requires emotional maturity.

You must learn to understand your emotions without being controlled by them.

You must learn to identify what triggers you and why.

You must learn to communicate with clarity rather than frustration.

You must learn how to navigate conflict without compromising your character.

Emotion is not the enemy. Unmanaged emotion is.

Mastery does not silence emotion.

Mastery interprets emotion.

Mastery uses emotion as information rather than justification.

As you grow deeper into mastery, you begin to understand that your mind is the engine of your leadership. If your inner world is fragmented, your leadership will be inconsistent. If your inner world is stable, your leadership will be steady. Mastery creates the stability needed to navigate leadership at a high level. It trains you to respond with wisdom rather than react with fear. It allows you to see situations with clarity rather than through the lens of insecurity. It gives you the strength to lead others because you have first learned to lead yourself.

Mastery requires you to guard your environment. Not every voice deserves access to your mind. Not every conversation deserves a response. Not every opportunity deserves your energy. As you rise, your standards must rise with you. You must be intentional about who you allow to influence your thinking. You must be aware of the people who support your growth and the people who quietly weaken it. Your inner world cannot thrive in an environment that contradicts your purpose.

Mastery also invites you to develop resilience. Resilience is not the ability to avoid difficulty. It is the ability to endure difficulty without losing your direction. Mastery teaches you that difficulty does not define you. It refines you. It sharpens your focus. It strengthens your identity. It clarifies your values. Resilience is created in the moments where you choose to rise rather than retreat, to learn rather than collapse, to move forward rather than settle where you are.

Mastery is a lifestyle. It is the commitment to becoming grounded, intentional, spiritually anchored, emotionally mature, and mentally strong. It is the daily decision to protect your purpose. It is the ongoing discipline of living with clarity. It is the humility to keep learning even as you grow. It is the wisdom to stay aligned even as you evolve.

The leader who masters their inner world becomes unstoppable in their outer world.

This is the beginning of your mastery.

This is where your leadership becomes a force of stability, clarity, and purpose.

This is where you step fully into the life you were created to live.

This is where you begin to become the sum in its highest form.

Chapter 31 SUM IT UP

THE SUM FRAMEWORK: SEE + UNDERSTAND + MANIFEST

Your future opens when your faith becomes stronger than your fear.

SEE: the opportunities God has placed before you.

UNDERSTAND: the growth required to walk into them.

MANIFEST: faith by taking bold steps.

BECOMING THE SUM:

1. What opportunity is calling you?

2. What fear is connected to it?

3. What step shows your readiness?

THE SUM CHALLENGE:

Say yes to one opportunity you've avoided out of fear.

PRAYER FOR THE JOURNEY:

God, strengthen my faith and help me step boldly into what You are opening for me. Amen.

"Legacy is both burden and blessing. You must carry it with intention."

CHAPTER 32

THE WEIGHT AND GIFT OF LEGACY

Legacy begins in the quiet decisions you make long before anyone sees the impact. It begins in the way you show up when no one is watching. It begins in the way you treat people you do not need. It begins in the standards you hold for yourself when convenience offers an easier path. Legacy is not a future accomplishment. Legacy is a present responsibility.

Most people think legacy is measured in achievements or accolades. They imagine it as something external, something the world eventually recognizes. But legacy is first an internal reality. It is the imprint your character leaves on every environment you enter. It is the strength of your presence. It is the consistency of your integrity. It is the love you give. It is the wisdom you share. It is the stability you create. Legacy is not built in a single moment. It is built in the accumulation of the choices you make daily.

Legacy becomes clear when you start to understand that your life has consequences. Not negative consequences, but meaningful ones. The person you are becoming will shape more than your career. It will shape the emotional climate of your home. It will shape the self-esteem of your children. It will shape the confidence of the people you lead. It will shape the culture of your teams and communities. The decisions you make today will ripple through the lives of people you may never meet. That is the weight and gift of legacy.

Legacy also requires humility. It asks you to acknowledge that the world is bigger than your personal goals. It asks you to recognize that your growth is not only for you. It is for the people who will learn from you, follow you, and trust you. It is for the people who will never know your name but will benefit from your influence. Legacy asks you to carry your purpose with maturity because your life is connected to lives you were meant to impact.

Legacy demands intention. It requires you to ask meaningful questions about who you are becoming and what your life is shaping. You must ask yourself whether your actions reflect your values. You must examine whether your habits support the kind of leader you hope to be remembered as. You must evaluate the environments you create through your words, your presence, and your decisions. Legacy is not an accident. It is intentionality expressed over time.

Legacy teaches you to pay attention to the invisible moments. The moments you choose patience over reaction. The moments you choose honesty over comfort. The moments you choose compassion over judgment. The moments you choose growth over familiarity. These moments reveal the depth of your character. They reveal whether your leadership is performative or authentic. They reveal whether your influence is temporary or transformative.

Legacy also invites you to think generationally. It pushes you to ask what you are building for the people who will come after you. It encourages you to mentor, teach, support, and model what is possible. It compels you to speak life into others, to help them rise, and to create opportunities for them to grow. Legacy is built through empowerment.

A true leader lifts people, not because it benefits them, but because it elevates the world.

Legacy becomes powerful when it aligns with purpose. When your life is rooted in meaning, your influence becomes more than success. It becomes significance. Purpose shapes your decisions so that what you leave behind is not accidental. It becomes a reflection of your spiritual alignment, your emotional maturity, your character, your sacrifice, and your willingness to become the highest version of yourself.

There will be moments where life reminds you of the fragility of time. You will see people you love leave this world too soon. You will experience loss that sharpens your awareness of your own purpose. You will witness others struggle, and it will push you to become someone who brings stability, guidance, compassion, and truth into the lives of those who need it. Legacy grows in those moments. It grows when you realize that your strength can prevent someone else from falling. It grows when your wisdom protects someone else from pain. It grows when your story becomes a bridge for someone else to cross into hope.

Legacy asks you to consider what you want your life to mean. What values you want to embody. What message you want your actions to communicate. What memories you want to leave in the hearts of the people around you. Legacy is not about the end of your life. It is about the quality of your life now. It is about living with such conviction that your presence becomes a standard for excellence, compassion, and purpose.

Legacy is not the story people tell about you.

Legacy is the life your presence inspires others to live.

It is the lasting imprint of your choices, your leadership, your heart, and your becoming.

This is the chapter where you shift from living for today to living for generations.

This is where your influence deepens.

This is where your purpose expands.

This is where you begin to build the world your life will leave behind.

This is where you continue to become the sum.

Chapter 32 SUM IT UP

THE SUM FRAMEWORK: SEE + UNDERSTAND + MANIFEST

Your thoughts shape your direction. Renew your mind and your life follows.

SEE: the thoughts that limit your confidence.

UNDERSTAND: why they remain.

MANIFEST: a renewed mindset with daily discipline.

BECOMING THE SUM:

1. What thought has limited you?

2. What truth replaces it?

3. What new thought can you practice today?

THE SUM CHALLENGE:

Speak one renewed thought over yourself today.

PRAYER FOR THE JOURNEY:

God, renew my thinking and anchor my mind in truth. Amen.

"You are the sum of all you endured, all you healed, and all you rose into."

CHAPTER 33

BECOMING THE SUM

There comes a point in a person's journey where everything they have lived through, learned from, fought for, and risen above begins to make sense. Not because life suddenly becomes easy, but because you start to see the design in what once felt disconnected. You begin to understand that your experiences were never isolated moments. They were pieces of a larger becoming. Every difficult season. Every unexpected shift. Every quiet victory. Every unspoken prayer. Every moment you survived when you did not know how. All of it was preparing you for who you are capable of becoming.

Becoming the sum is the recognition that nothing in your life was wasted. The pain, the healing, the losses, the breakthroughs, the waiting, the rebuilding, the growth, the lessons, the seasons you outgrew, the habits you left behind, the environments you walked away from, the people who shaped you, the people who tested you, the moments that sharpened you, and the moments that humbled you. Each one contributed something meaningful to your development. Each one added something to your identity. Each one strengthened a part of you that leadership would eventually require.

Becoming the sum is not about perfection. It is about wholeness. It is about integrating the many parts of your story into a unified identity. It is about accepting every chapter of your life without letting any single chapter define you. It is about recognizing that you are not shaped by a single experience, but by the full weight of your becoming. The strength you carry now is the accumulated force of everything you have risen through.

As you reach this point in your journey, you begin to understand that leadership is not a role you perform. It is an identity you embody. It is the maturity to stand in your purpose even when life feels uncertain. It is the courage to lead others with compassion because you have known pain. It is the discipline to stay consistent because you have known chaos. It is the humility to keep learning because you have known times when you thought you had it all figured out. Becoming the sum means you draw from every lesson, every failure, every success, and every moment of grace that shaped your character.

Becoming the sum also requires acceptance. You must accept that your past cannot be altered, but it can be used. You must accept that healing is not linear but necessary. You must accept that growth is uncomfortable but transformative. You must accept that leadership will require more from you than you expected but give more back to you than you imagined. Acceptance does not mean surrender. Acceptance means alignment. It means stepping into the fullness of who you are with clarity rather than denial.

Becoming the sum means you stop carrying your past as a burden and begin carrying it as wisdom. You stop hiding the parts of your story that once made you feel less worthy. You stop judging yourself for moments you were not prepared for. You stop diminishing your strength to make others comfortable. Becoming the sum means you recognize that the leader you are today is a product of your resilience, not your perfection. You are not here by accident. You are here because you survived what tried to break you and grew from what tried to limit you.

As you continue to rise, you will begin to notice how becoming the sum influences those around you. Your presence becomes grounding. Your leadership becomes steady. Your compassion becomes deeper. Your boundaries become clearer. Your vision becomes stronger. You begin to lead from a place of maturity rather than fear, purpose rather than pressure, conviction rather than insecurity. People feel the stability in you because you have learned how to stabilize yourself. People trust your guidance because you have learned how to guide your own transformation.

Becoming the sum does not remove struggle. It strengthens you to navigate it with wisdom and dignity. It does not remove pain. It teaches you how to heal without losing your identity. It does not eliminate uncertainty. It anchors you so deeply in purpose that uncertainty can no longer take your direction from you. Becoming the sum turns adversity into refinement. It turns loss into empathy. It turns learning into purpose. It turns faith into clarity.

Take a moment and reflect on the journey you have walked through. Consider the version of yourself who began this book. The one who carried questions, doubts, or weight you did not yet have language for. Now consider the version of yourself who stands here. Someone who has grown. Someone who has become more aware of their identity. Someone who has confronted their thoughts, strengthened their habits, refined their mindset, elevated their environment, and invested in the person they are becoming. This is becoming the sum in real time.

As you move forward, your responsibility is to protect the identity you have built. To live with intention. To honor the lessons that shaped you. To lead with courage. To love with depth. To carry your purpose with clarity. To rise into the version of yourself that your future requires. Becoming the sum is not a destination. It is a lifelong posture. It is the ongoing commitment to integrate everything you have gained into everything you are becoming.

Before you turn the page to the closing chapter of this book, pause. Breathe. Honor your growth. Reflect on what you have learned.

You have walked through fire.

You have risen from difficulty.

You have grown through purpose.

You have aligned your identity with the future you desire.

This chapter marks not the end of your transformation but the unveiling of who you were designed to be.

This is becoming the sum.

Chapter 33 SUM IT UP

THE SUM FRAMEWORK: SEE + UNDERSTAND + MANIFEST

You have matured. You have healed. You have grown. Stand in the identity God built in you.

SEE: the leader you have become.

UNDERSTAND: the strength and wisdom that guide you now.

MANIFEST: legacy through confident leadership.

BECOMING THE SUM:

1. Who are you now compared to who you were?

2. What growth are you most proud of?

3. How will you lead differently from this place of maturity?

THE SUM CHALLENGE:

Lead today from the identity you earned through growth.

PRAYER FOR THE JOURNEY:

God, thank You for the transformation in my life. Guide my steps as I step into the leader You created me to be. Amen.

"A leader's greatest work is not the life they live, but the lives they awaken."

EPILOGUE

There is a moment at the end of every journey where the path becomes yours alone. Not because you are meant to walk it isolated, but because no one can take the steps that belong to you. People can inspire you. They can teach you. They can encourage you. They can guide you. But eventually, the responsibility to rise becomes personal. The responsibility to grow becomes sacred. The responsibility to step into the life you were created for becomes yours to honor.

You are reaching that moment now.

Everything you have lived, survived, learned, questioned, released, strengthened, and rebuilt has prepared you for this season. You are no longer reading from the posture of who you used to be. You are reading from the posture of who you are. You carry more clarity. More awareness. More discipline. More courage. More vision. More truth. More purpose. That is not accidental. That is the evidence of your becoming.

The next chapter of your life will not be written by your fears. It will be written by your decisions. It will be written by your standards. It will be written by your self-leadership. It will be written by the moments where you choose purpose over comfort and growth over familiarity. You are now responsible for the future you once only imagined. That future is not waiting for someone else. It is waiting for you.

You are equipped.

You are prepared.

You are capable.

You are called.

The world does not need your perfection.

The world needs your presence.

Your leadership.

Your empathy.

Your wisdom.

Your resilience.

Your voice.

Your courage.

Your story.

There will be days ahead where doubt returns. There will be days where old patterns attempt to reappear. There will be days where the weight of life feels heavier than you expected. Do not mistake those moments for failure. They are invitations. Invitations to remember what you have learned. Invitations to apply what you have strengthened. Invitations to lead yourself the way you were created to lead others. You are no longer the person who collapses under pressure. You are the person who rises with purpose.

You may not realize it yet, but someone's clarity is tied to your courage. Someone's hope is tied to your healing. Someone's breakthrough is tied to your consistency. Someone's direction is tied to your leadership. Someone's faith is tied to your example. You are a carrier of change. You are a vessel of possibility. You are the sum of everything you have overcome and the potential of everything you are yet to become.

As you leave these pages and step into your next chapter, I pray you move with boldness.

Boldness to speak truth.

Boldness to show compassion.

Boldness to set boundaries.

Boldness to lead with integrity.

Boldness to honor your purpose.

Boldness to build the life you were created to live.

Boldness to become the sum in every season.

May God strengthen your hands, steady your steps, guard your mind, and guide your path.

May your life continue to expand with clarity and direction.

May the work you do transform the lives entrusted to your leadership.

May you rise into the fullness of who you are called to be.

May the legacy you build reflect the depth of your values and the power of your healing.

May your story become evidence that transformation is possible, purpose is real, and leadership is sacred.

This book was never meant to entertain you.

It was meant to awaken you.

It was meant to grow you.

It was meant to prepare you.

It was meant to activate you.

Now the pages end, but your journey does not.

You are walking into the next season with intention, strength, truth, identity, and purpose.

You are ready.

You are worthy.

You are equipped.

You are the sum.

And now, it is your turn.

THE CHARGE TO THE READER

Your life has been preparing you for something sacred.

Your experiences have been shaping your insight.

Your struggles have been strengthening your capacity.

Your growth has been expanding your influence.

Your faith has been anchoring your purpose.

So here is the charge:

Step fully into the leader you are.

Stop shrinking to fit environments you have outgrown.

Stop waiting for permission to walk in your calling.

Stop telling the old story when your life is ready for a new one.

Stop carrying burdens that God already asked you to release.

Do not let your past convince you that your purpose is small.

You are called to lead.

You are called to influence.

You are called to heal.

You are called to build.

You are called to make a difference.

What you do next matters.

FINAL BLESSING & PRAYER

May God strengthen you for the road ahead. May He heal the parts of your story that still feel heavy. May He remind you that you are chosen, seen, and called. May He expand your vision beyond what you imagined for yourself. May He align you with people who sharpen your growth and honor your purpose. May He give you courage to step into the next chapter of your life with confidence. May He protect your peace, your family, your mind, and your mission. May He restore what was lost, rebuild what was broken, and renew what was forgotten. May He place you exactly where your leadership is needed most. And may you never forget:

Your life has meaning.

Your story has power.

Your calling has weight.

Your journey matters.

Amen.

ACKNOWLEDGMENTS

Becoming the sum has never been a solitary journey. My growth has been shaped by countless people whose presence, guidance, and belief left a lasting imprint on my life. I am grateful for every one of you.

To the mentors, coaches, teachers, instructors, and leaders who invested time, wisdom, correction, and clarity into my development. Thank you for seeing potential when life was still teaching me how to recognize it in myself. Your influence helped form the standards and discipline that anchor my leadership today.

To every Soldier, teammate, sister and brother I served beside. Thank you for trusting my leadership in moments that demanded strength, integrity, and unwavering focus. You shaped my understanding of responsibility and the weight of influence in ways that no classroom ever could.

To every student, young person, athlete, community member, and individual I have had the honor to teach, support, or mentor. You taught me how to lead with empathy. You reminded me that people rise not because they are pushed, but because they are believed in. Your lives are the reason I continue to serve with intention.

To those who supported me during seasons of transition, loss, uncertainty, or rebuilding. Your presence gave me strength I did not always have words for. Thank you for standing with me when life required more of me than I expected.

To my colleagues and communities who encouraged my voice, challenged my thinking, and respected my purpose. Thank you for giving me space to grow and room to lead.

To the readers of this book. Thank you for opening your heart to these pages and allowing my journey to speak into yours. Thank you for your willingness to grow, reflect, and rise. You are the reason this book exists. Your courage, your honesty, and your becoming give this work meaning.

Above all, I acknowledge God for being the source of every insight, every lesson, every page, and every moment that shaped this book. His guidance carried me. His presence sustained me. His purpose continues to unfold through every part of my journey.

To everyone who has influenced, strengthened, challenged, or supported me in any way, thank you. Your fingerprints are on every chapter.

AUTHOR'S NOTE

Thank you for walking with me through this book.

Every chapter was written with hope, humility, and a deep belief in the potential that lives within you. I pray that something in these pages reminded you of your strength, affirmed your identity, or awakened your purpose.

This book is not the end of the story.

It is an invitation.

An invitation to lead yourself with honesty.

To lead others with compassion.

To build a life that reflects the fullness of who you are.

To live as the sum of your experiences, not the shadow of them.

To step into the world as a leader shaped by truth, vision, healing, and faith.

If this book touched you, challenged you, encouraged you, or changed you,

then its purpose has been fulfilled.

Your journey continues.

Your influence is needed.

Your purpose is calling.

Lead with courage.

Lead with clarity.

Lead with conviction.

Lead with love.

And always remember:

You were created for this.

ABOUT THE AUTHOR

ElDon White is a leadership architect whose life's work transforms adversity into generational possibility. Forged through hardship and sharpened in purpose, he has spent his career guiding others from survival into identity, alignment, and impact.

With over twenty-one years of service in the U.S. Military, including historic roles as the first Geospatial Engineer to successfully serve in the 75th Ranger Regiment, a senior NCO within Joint Special Operations Command, and the Department of Defense first enlisted active duty executive coach, ElDon has shaped leaders in some of the most demanding environments in the world. His career built a foundation of presence, purpose, and transformational influence.

Today, he serves as co-founder of Xponential Growth Academy LLC, where he and his wife, Dr. Laurine LeBlanc-White, integrate leadership development, emotional intelligence, trauma-informed coaching, mental health counseling and faith-centered guidance for global audiences. Their mission extends from schools to corporations to international platforms, helping people unlock the leader within and rise into their God-given assignment.

A speaker, coach, strategist, and mentor to leaders across sectors, ElDon is committed to expanding what is possible for the underrepresented and elevating those called to serve and lead.

His purpose is simple: awaken identity, ignite purpose, and build leaders who transform generations.

"I am a black leader. I am excellence. I embody black leadership. I am the SUM of my past and future experiences. I lead as a SUM leader."

https://www.xponential-growth.com